Data Science with Raspberry Pi

Real-Time Applications Using a Localized Cloud

K. Mohaideen Abdul Kadhar
G. Anand

Apress®

Data Science with Raspberry Pi: Real-Time Applications Using a Localized Cloud

K. Mohaideen Abdul Kadhar
Pollachi, Tamil Nadu, India

G. Anand
Pollachi, Tamil Nadu, India

ISBN-13 (pbk): 978-1-4842-6824-7
https://doi.org/10.1007/978-1-4842-6825-4

ISBN-13 (electronic): 978-1-4842-6825-4

Managing Director, Apress Media LLC: Welmoed Spahr
Acquisitions Editor: Aaron Black
Development Editor: Matthew Moodie
Coordinating Editor: Jessica Vakili

Distributed to the book trade worldwide by Springer Science+Business Media New York, 233 Spring Street, 6th Floor, New York, NY 10013. Phone 1-800-SPRINGER, fax (201) 348-4505, e-mail orders-ny@springer-sbm.com, or visit www.springeronline.com. Apress Media, LLC is a California LLC and the sole member (owner) is Springer Science + Business Media Finance Inc (SSBM Finance Inc). SSBM Finance Inc is a Delaware corporation.

For information on translations, please e-mail booktranslations@springernature.com; for reprint, paperback, or audio rights, please e-mail bookpermissions@springernature.com.

Apress titles may be purchased in bulk for academic, corporate, or promotional use. eBook versions and licenses are also available for most titles. For more information, reference our Print and eBook Bulk Sales web page at www.apress.com/bulk-sales.

Any source code or other supplementary material referenced by the author in this book is available to readers on GitHub via the book's product page, located at www.apress.com/978-1-4842-6824-7. For more detailed information, please visit www.apress.com/source-code.

Printed on acid-free paper

To my wife Jashima for her support in writing this book.

—Dr. K. Mohaideen Abdul Kadhar

To my parents for their continuous encouragement in writing this book.

—G. Anand

Table of Contents

About the Authors

Dr. K. Mohaideen Abdul Kadhar earned an undergraduate degree in electronics and communication engineering and a master of technology degree with a specialization in control and instrumentation. In 2015, he obtained his PhD in control system design using evolutionary algorithms. He has more than 14 years of experience in teaching and research. His areas of interest are evolutionary algorithms, control systems, signal processing and computer vision. Now, He is working to implement signal processing and control system concepts with Python programming on the Raspberry Pi. He has taught many courses and has delivered workshops about data science with Python programming. In addition, he has acted as a consultant for many industries in developing machine vision systems for industrial applications.

G. Anand obtained his bachelor of engineering degree in electronics and communication engineering in 2008 and his master of engineering degree in communication systems in 2011. He has more than nine years of teaching experience with a specialization in signal and image processing. He has taught courses and acted as a resource person in workshops related to Python programming. His current research focus is in the domain of artificial intelligence and machine learning.

About the Technical Reviewer

Maris Sekar is a professional computer engineer, certified information systems auditor (ISACA), and senior data scientist (Data Science Council of America). He has a passion for using storytelling to drive better decision-making and operational efficiencies. Maris has cross-functional work experience in various domains such as risk management, data analytics, and strategy.

Acknowledgments

First, I wish to thank the almighty Allah for giving me strength and courage in writing this book. Writing a book is more complex than I thought. We struggled many times when developing the content of this book because this book focuses not only the concepts but also on the real-time implementation details on the Raspberry Pi.

My sincere thanks to my family, especially my mom and dad. Without them, I would not have attained this level of achievement.

A very special thanks to my wife Mrs. M. Jashima Parveen for her support and love. She always set me free for writing this book. In my hard times, her support and encouragement gave me strength and courage. I could not have done it without her.

My sincere thanks to chief editor Mr. Aaron Black and book coordinator Ms. Jessica Vakkili for their enormous support. Even when some of the chapters were delayed, they gave their support in developing the contents of the book.

My heartfelt thanks to the management of Dr. Mahalingam College of Engineering and Technology, Pollachi, especially, I thank to my Head of the Department, Dr. R. Sudhakar, Professor, for his encouragement and trust in my work and knowledge.

Last but not least, special thanks to my colleague G. Anand for his support and coordination in writing the book.

Introduction

In modern times data can be thought of as a valuable commodity like oil or gold because we can get a lot of useful information from data with the help of some scientific methods, and we can make intelligent decisions based on that information and convert it into money. *Data science* is the process of extracting knowledge/useful information from the data.

For example, IBM forecasted that the demand for skilled people in data science will increase by 28 percent in 2020. Many industries use data science concepts in different aspects of their business such as checking whether they have achieved their targets, finding the root cause of failures, etc. Recently, data science has been effectively implemented in politics to develop strategies, identify the weak regions, predict the emotions and expectations of the people, etc. Further, local governments utilize the data collected from the people of their town to devise the planning and policies for the development of the town. Data science is also successfully applied in the agricultural domain in areas like drought assessment, crops yield and remote sensing, etc. This shows that the applications related to data science concepts are emerging nowadays across multiple domains.

Most of the recent books have focused on applying data science techniques to some open and standard dataset. This book is specifically about applying data science concepts in the Raspberry Pi board. The Raspberry Pi can act as a single on board computer and can also interact with the real-time environment via sensors as most of the local servers can't do this task.

The book will start with a brief introduction to data science followed by which there will be a dedicated chapter for explaining the concepts of Python starting from the installation of the software to the various

data types and modules available. The next two chapters will introduce
the readers to Raspberry Pi devices, their hardware description, and
the setting up of the devices for gathering real-time data. The next four
chapters will deal with the different operations in data science with respect
to real time applications using Raspberry Pi hardware. The penultimate
chapter of the book will discuss about the concepts that will enable the
Raspberry Pi to learn from the data. The last chapter will have few case
studies that will give the readers an idea of the range of domains where
these concepts can be applied.

CHAPTER 1

Introduction to Data Science

Data is a collection of information in the form of words, numbers, and descriptions about the subject. Consider the following statement: "The dog has four legs, is 1.5m high, and has brown hair." This statement has three different kinds of information (i.e., data) about the dog. The data "four" and "1.5m" is numerical data, and "brown hair" is descriptive. It is good to know the various kinds of data types to understand the data, perform effective analysis, and better extract knowledge from the data. Basically, data can be categorized into two types.

- Quantitative data
- Qualitative data

Quantitative data can be obtained only with the help of measurements and not through observations. This can be represented in the form of numerical values. Quantitative data can be further classified into continuous and discrete. The exact integer values are *discrete* data, whereas *continuous* data can be any value in a range. *Qualitative data* is a description of the characteristics of a subject. Usually qualitative data can be obtained from observations and cannot be measured. In other words, qualitative data may be described as categorical data, and quantitative data can be called numerical data.

© K. Mohaideen Abdul Kadhar and G. Anand 2021
K. M. Abdul Kadhar and G. Anand, *Data Science with Raspberry Pi*,
https://doi.org/10.1007/978-1-4842-6825-4_1

For example, in the previous statement, "brown hair" describes a characteristic of the dog and is qualitative data, whereas "four legs" and "1.5m" are the quantitative data and are categorized as discrete and continuous data, respectively.

Data can be available in structured and unstructured form. When the data is organized in a predefined data model/structure, it is called *structured data*. Structured data can be stored in a tabular format or a relational database with the help of query languages. We can also store this kind of data in an Excel file format, like the student database given in Table 1-1.

Table 1-1. *An Example of Structured Data*

Student Roll Number	Marks	Attendance	Batch	Sex
111401	492/500	98%	2011-2014	Male
111402	442/500	72%	2011-2014	Male
121501	465/500	82%	2012-2015	Female
121502	452/500	87%	2012-2015	Male

Most human-generated and machine-generated data are unstructured data such as emails, documents, text files, log files, text messages, images, video and audio files, messages on the Web and social media, and data from sensors. This data can be converted to a structured format only through human or machine intervention. Figure 1-1 shows the various sources of unstructured data.

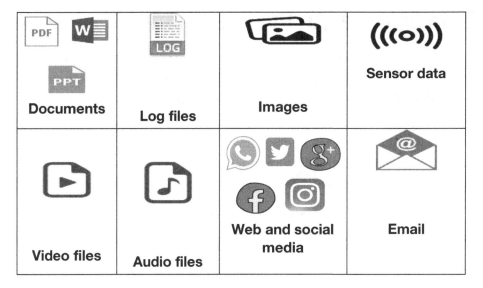

Figure 1-1. *Sources of unstructured data*

Importance of Data Types in Data Science

Before starting to analyze data, it is important to know about the data types so you can choose the suitable analysis methods. The analysis of continuous data is different from the analysis of categorical data; hence, using the same analysis methods for both may lead to incorrect analysis.

For example, in statistical analysis where continuous data is involved, the probability of an exact event is zero, while the result can be different for discrete data.

You can also choose the visualization tools based on the data types. For instance, continuous data is usually represented using histograms, whereas discrete data can be visualized with the help of bar charts.

Data Science: An Overview

As discussed at the beginning of the chapter, data science is nothing but the extraction of knowledge or information from the data. Unfortunately, not all data gives useful information. It is based on the client requirements, the hypothesis, the nature of the data type, and the methods used for analysis and modeling. Therefore, a few processes are required before analyzing or modeling the data for intelligent decision-making. Figure 1-2 describes these data science processes.

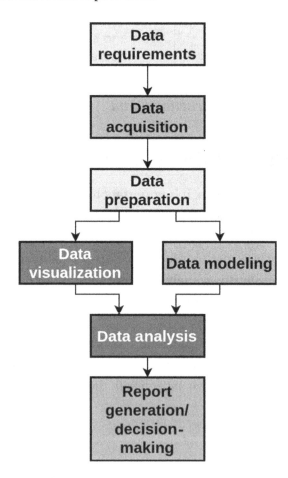

Figure 1-2. *Data science process*

Data Requirements

To develop a data science project, the data scientists first understand the problem based on the client/business requirements and then define the objectives of the problem for analysis. For example, say a client wants to analyze the emotion of people on a government policy. First, the objectives of the problem can be set as "To collect the opinion of the people about the government policy." Then, the data scientists decide on the kind of data that can support the objective and the resources of data. For the example problem, the possible data is social media data, including text messages and opinion polls of various categories of people, with information about their education level, age, occupation, etc. Before starting the data collection, a good work plan is essential for collecting the data from various sources. Setting the objectives and work plan can reduce the time spent collecting the data and can help to prepare the report.

Data Acquisition

There are many types of structured open data available on the internet that we call *secondary data*, because that kind of data is collected by somebody and structured into some tabular format. If the user wants to collect the data directly from a source, that is called *primary data*. Initially, the unstructured data is collected via many resources such as mobile devices, emails, sensors, cameras, direct interaction with people, video files, audio files, text messages, blogs, etc.

Data Preparation

Data preparation is the most important part of the data science process. Preparing the data puts the data into proper form for knowledge extraction. There are three steps in the data preparation stage.

1. Data processing

2. Data cleaning

3. Data transformation

Data Processing

This step is important as it is required to check the quality of data while we import it from various sources. This quality checking is done to ensure that the data is in the correct data type, standard format, and has no typos or errors in the variables. This step will reduce data issues when doing analysis. Moreover, in this phase, the collected unstructured data can be organized in the form of structured data for analysis and visualization.

Data Cleaning

Once the data processing is done, cleaning the data is required as the data might still have some errors. These errors will affect the actual information present in the data. Possible errors are as follows:

- Duplicates

- Human or machine errors

- Missing values

- Outliers

- Inappropriate values

Duplicates

In the database, some data is repeated multiple times, which results in *duplicates*. It is better to check and remove the duplicates to reduce the overhead in computation during data analysis.

Human or Machine Errors

The data is collected from sources either by humans or by machines. Some errors are inevitable during this process due to human carelessness or machine failure. The possible solution to avoid these kinds of errors is to match the variables and values with standard ones.

Missing Values

While converting the unstructured data into a structured form, some rows and columns may not have any values (i.e., empty). This error will cause discontinuity in the information and make it difficult to visualize it. There are many built-in functions available in programming languages we can use to check if the data has any missing values.

Outliers

In statistics, an outlier is a data point that differs significantly from other observations. An outlier may be because of variability in the measurement or it may indicate experimental errors; outliers are sometimes excluded from the data set. Figure 1-3 shows an example of outlier data. Outlier data can cause problems with certain types of models, which in turn will influence the decision-making.

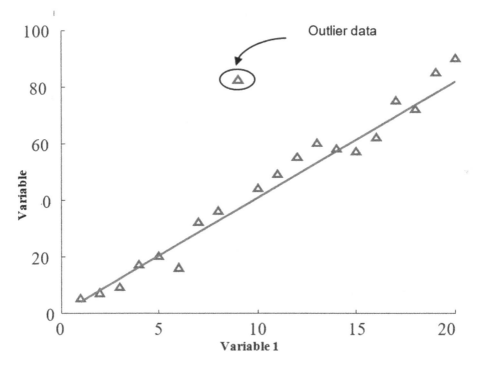

Figure 1-3. *Outlier data*

Transforming the Data

Data transformation can be done by many methods using normalization, min-max operations, correlation information, etc.

Data Visualization

Based on the requirements of the user, the data can be analyzed with the help of visualization tools such as charts, graphs, etc. These visualization tools help people to understand the trends, variations, and deviations in a particular variable in the data set. Visualization techniques can be used as a part of exploratory data analysis.

Data Analysis

The data can be further analyzed with the help of mathematical techniques such as statistical techniques. The improvements, deviations, and variations are determined in a numerical form. We can also generate an analysis report by combining the results of visualization tools and analysis techniques.

Modeling and Algorithms

Today many machine learning algorithms are employed to predict useful information from raw data. For example, neural networks can be used to identify the users who are willing to donate funds to orphans based on the users' previous behavior. In this scenario, the previous behavior data of users can be collected based on their education, activities, occupation, sex, etc. The neural network can be trained with this collected data. Whenever a new user's data is fed to this model, it can predict whether the new user will give funds or not. However, the accuracy of the prediction is based on the reliability and the amount of data used while training.

There are many machine learning algorithms available such as regression techniques, support vector machine (SVM), neural networks, deep neural networks, recurrent neural networks, etc., that can be applied to data modeling. After data modeling, the model can be analyzed by giving data from new users and developing a prediction report.

Report Generation/Decision-Making

Finally, a report can be developed based on the analysis with the help of visualization tools, mathematical or statistical techniques, and models. Such reports can be helpful in many circumstances such as forecasting the strengths and weakness of an organization, industry, government, etc.

The facts and findings from the report can make the decisions quite easy and intelligent. Moreover, the analysis report can be generated automatically using some automation tools based on the client requirements.

Recent Trends in Data Science

Certain fields in data science are growing exponentially and therefore will be attractive to data scientists. They are discussed in the following sections.

Automation in Data Science

In the current scenario, data science still needs a lot of manual work such as data processing, data cleaning, and transforming the data. These steps consume a lot of time and computations. The modern world demands the automation of data science processes such as data processing, data cleaning, data transformations, analysis, visualization, and report generation. Hence, the automation field will be a top demand in the data science industry.

Artificial Intelligence–Based Data Analyst

Artificial intelligence techniques and machine learning algorithms can be implemented effectively for modeling the data. Particularly, reinforcement learning with deep neural networks is used to upgrade the learning of the model based on variations in the data. Also, machine learning techniques can be used for automated data science projects.

Cloud Computing

The amount of data used by people nowadays has increased exponentially. Some industries gather a large amount of data every day and hence find it difficult to store and analyze with the help of local servers. This makes it expensive in terms of computation and maintenance. So, they prefer cloud computing in which the data can be stored on cloud servers and can be retrieved anytime and anywhere for analysis. Many cloud computing companies offer a data analytics platform on their cloud servers. The more growth in data processing, the more this field will gain attention.

Edge Computing

Many small-scale industries don't require the analysis of data on cloud servers and instead require analysis reports instantly. For these kinds of applications, edge devices can be a possible solution to acquire the data, analyze it, and present a report in visual form or numerical form instantly to the users. In the future, the requirements of edge computing will increase significantly.

Natural Language Processing

Natural language processing (NLP) can be used to extract unstructured data from websites, emails, servers, log files, etc. In addition, NLP can be useful for converting text into a single data format. For example, we can convert people's emotion into a data format from their messages on social media. This will be a powerful tool for collecting data from many sources, and its demand will continue to increase.

Why Data Science on the Raspberry Pi?

Many books explain the different processes involved in data science in relation to cloud computing. But in this book, the concepts of data science will be discussed as part of real-time applications using the Raspberry Pi. The Raspberry Pi boards can interact with the real-time world by connecting to a wide range of sensors using their general-purpose input/output (GPIO) pins, which makes it easier to collect real-time data. Owing to their small size and low cost, a number of nodes of these Raspberry Pi boards can be connected as a network, thereby enabling localized operation. In other words, the Raspberry Pi can be used as an edge computing device for data processing and storage, closer to the devices used for acquiring the information and thereby overcoming the disadvantages associated with cloud computing. Therefore, a lot of data processing applications can be implemented using a distribution of these devices that can manage real-time data and run the analytics locally. This book will help you to implement real-time data science applications using the Raspberry Pi.

CHAPTER 2

Basics of Python Programming

Python is a general-purpose dynamic programming language that was created by Dutch programmer Guido van Rossum in 1989. It is the most commonly used programming language in the field of data science. Since it is easier to learn and write code in Python than other languages, it is an optimal choice for beginners. The widespread use of Python is also attributed to the fact that it is free and open source. The number of scientific libraries and packages developed by the Python community allows for data scientists to work with data-intensive real-time applications. Some of the leading organizations such as Google, Dropbox, and Netflix are using Python at various levels to enhance their software. In this chapter, we will discuss Python installation on the Windows operating system, different Python IDEs, the fundamental data types available with Python, control flow statements, Python functions, and different Python libraries for data science.

© K. Mohaideen Abdul Kadhar and G. Anand 2021
K. M. Abdul Kadhar and G. Anand, *Data Science with Raspberry Pi*,
https://doi.org/10.1007/978-1-4842-6825-4_2

Why Python?

Python is the most preferred programming language for data scientists because of the following reasons:

- It is an open source programming language with a strong and growing community of contributors and users.

- It has a simpler syntax than other programming languages such as C, C++, and Java.

- It allows users to perform object-oriented programming.

- It has a large set of libraries that can be used to perform a variety of tasks such as developing a website, building machine learning applications, etc.

- It can be used in embedded, small hardware devices like the Raspberry Pi that allows for real-time implementation of various applications.

Python Installation

Most distributions of the Linux operating system come with the preloaded Python package, but it has to be installed separately in the case of Windows operating system. The procedure to install Python on the Windows operating system is as follows:

1. Open a browser and go to Python.org, the official site for Python.

2. On that page, click the Downloads tab and download the latest version of the software on the resulting page.

3. Once the download is complete, open the installer package. In the installation wizard, shown in Figure 2-1, select Add Python to PATH, which will ensure that Python is added automatically to your system variable path; otherwise, this path must be added manually in the Environment Variables settings in your system.

4. Click Install Now to install the package.

Figure 2-1. *Installation wizard for Python*

After the installation is completed, you can verify the installation by typing *python --version* at the command prompt, which will display the version of Python installed on the system. If it does not show the version, then there could be a problem either with the installation or with the system path variable.

Refer to the Python documentation available on the official site to understand the procedure for downloading additional modules and packages for the software. Either you can start working with Python at the command prompt itself or you can install one among the various IDEs that are discussed in the next section.

Python IDEs

An *integrated development environment* (IDE) is a software suite that combines developer tools into a graphical user interface (GUI), which includes options for editing code and building, executing, and debugging programs. A number of IDEs are available for Python, each of which comes with its own advantages. Some of the commonly used IDEs are discussed here.

PyCharm

The PyCharm IDE was developed by the Czech company JetBrains. It is a cross-platform IDE that can be used on Windows, macOS, and Linux. It provides code analysis and a graphical debugger. It also supports web development with Django as well as data science with Anaconda. Some of the attractive features of PyCharm are the intelligent code completion, a simple package management interface, and the refactoring option, which provides the ability to make changes across multiple lines in a code.

Spyder

Spyder is a cross-platform IDE for scientific programming in the Python language. Spyder integrates with a number of scientific packages including NumPy, SciPy, Matplotlib, Pandas, IPython, and other open source software. It was released under the MIT license.

Jupyter Notebook

Jupyter Notebook is a web-based interactive computational environment. This notebook integrates code and its output in a single document that combines visualizations, text, mathematical equations, and other media thereby making it suitable for data science applications.

Python Programming with IDLE

IDLE is a simple cross-platform IDE suitable for beginners in an educational environment. It comes with features such as a multiwindow text editor, a Python shell with syntax highlighting, and an integrated debugger. Since this is a default editor that comes with Python, let's see how to execute Python code using IDLE.

There are two ways of executing the Python code in this IDLE. The first way is the interactive mode in which you can directly type the code next to the symbol >>> in the Python shell, as illustrated in Figure 2-2. Each line of code will be executed once you press Enter. The disadvantage of using the interactive mode is that when you save the code, it is saved along with the results, and this implies that you cannot use the saved code for execution later.

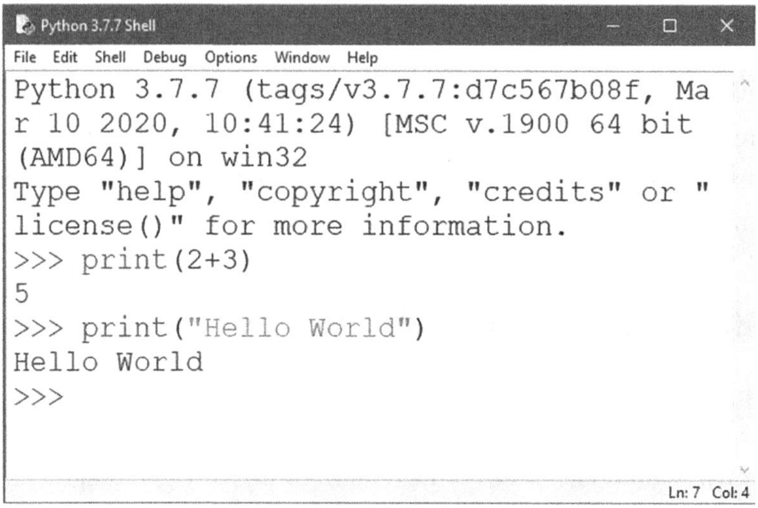

Figure 2-2. *Running Python code in interactive mode*

The second way is to run the code in script mode where you can open a script window and type the entire code there, which can then be saved with a .py extension to be used later. To open a script file window, go to the File menu at the top and click New File. In the script window, type the same two lines of code, shown in Figure 2-2. Figure 2-3 shows the script file window with the code. Then go to the File menu, click Save, and then save the program by specifying a proper filename. Ensure that the filename does not start with a number or have the same name as existing Python keywords.

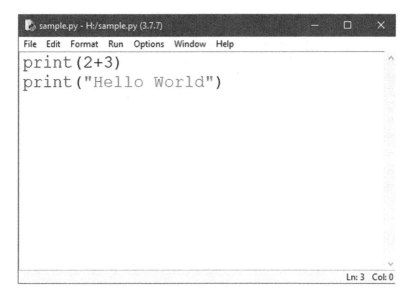

Figure 2-3. *Script file window*

Once the file is saved, the script can be executed by going to the Run menu at the top and clicking Run Module. This will execute the script and print the output in the Python shell, as shown in Figure 2-4.

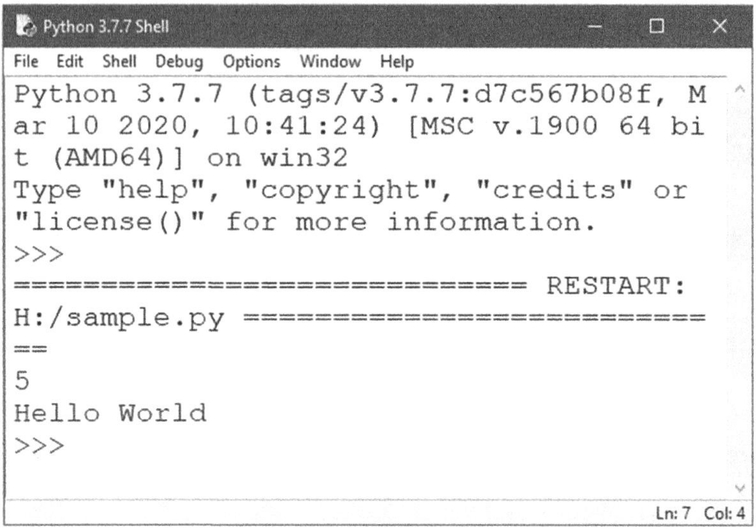

```
Python 3.7.7 Shell                                    —    □    ✕
File  Edit  Shell  Debug  Options  Window  Help
Python 3.7.7 (tags/v3.7.7:d7c567b08f, M
ar 10 2020, 10:41:24) [MSC v.1900 64 bi
t (AMD64)] on win32
Type "help", "copyright", "credits" or
"license()" for more information.
>>>
============================== RESTART:
H:/sample.py ===========================
==
5
Hello World
>>>
                                          Ln: 7  Col: 4
```

Figure 2-4. *Output of the script file*

Python Comments

Before we start to discuss the Python data types, it is essential to know about comment lines in Python as we will be using them often in our code. There are two ways to write comment lines based on the purpose of your comment.

If you intend to write a short comment, regarding a particular line in the code, for yourself, then single-line comments are the best choice. These single-line comments can be created by simply beginning the line with a hash (#) character, and they are terminated automatically by the end of the line. While executing the code, the Python compiler will ignore everything after the hash symbol up to the end of the line.

Multiple-line comments are intended to explain a particular aspect of your code to others and can be created by adding three single quotes (' ' ') at the beginning and end of the comment. The Python compiler will not ignore these comments, and they will appear in the output if your script has nothing else other than the comment. These two comments are illustrated using the IDLE Python shell format, as shown here:

```
>>> # This is a comment
>>> "'This is a comment"'
'This is a comment'
```

Python Data Types

A *data type*, in a programming language, is defined by the type of value that a variable can take. Python data types can be primarily classified into numeric and sequence data types. The data types that fall under these two categories are discussed in this section with relevant illustrations for each.

Numeric Data Types

Numeric data types are scalar variables that can take numeric values. The categories of numeric data types are int, float, and complex. In addition, we will discuss the bool data type that uses Boolean variables.

int

The int data type represents integers that are signed whole numbers without a decimal point. The code in Listing 2-1 displays the data type of an integer.

Listing 2-1. Integer Data Type

```
a=5
"'print the data type of variable a using type() funcion"'
print("a is of type",type(a))

Output:
a is of type <class 'int'>
```

float

The float data type represents floating-point numbers with a decimal point separating the integer and fractional parts. The code in Listing 2-2 prints the data type of a float value.

Listing 2-2. float Data Type

```
a = 5.0
print('a is of type',type(a))
```

```
Output:
a is of type <class 'float'>
```

complex

The complex data type represents complex numbers of the form *a+bj* where *a* and *b* are the real part and imaginary part, respectively. The numbers *a* and *b* may be either integers or floating-point numbers. The code in Listing 2-3 prints the data type of a complex number.

Listing 2-3. complex Data Type

```
a=3.5+4j
print('a is of type',type(a))
```

```
Output :
 a is of type <class 'complex'>
```

bool

In Python, Boolean variables are defined by True and False keywords. As Python is case sensitive, the keywords True and False must have an uppercase first letter. Listing 2-4 illustrates the bool data type.

Listing 2-4. bool Data Type

```
a= 8>9
print('a is of type',type(a))
print(a)
```

```
Output:
a is of type <class 'bool'>
False
```

Boolean values can be manipulated with Boolean operators, which include *and*, *or*, and *not*, as illustrated in Listing 2-5.

Listing 2-5. Manipulation of boolean Data Type

```
a = True
b = False
print(a or b)
```

```
Output:
True
```

Numeric Operators

Table 2-1 summarizes the numeric operations available in Python that can be applied to the numeric data types.

Table 2-1. *Numeric Operators in Python*

Operator	Operation
( )	Parentheses
**	Exponentiation
*	Multiplication
/	Division
+	Addition
-	Subtraction
%	Modulo operation

The operators in Table 2-1 are listed in their order of precedence. When more than one operation is performed in a particular line of your code, the order of execution will be according to the order of precedence in Table 2-1. Consider the example *2*3+5* where both multiplication and addition are involved. Since multiplication has higher precedence than addition, as observed from Table 2-1, the multiplication operator (*) will be executed first giving *2*3=6*, followed by the addition operator (+), which would give the final result of *6+5=11*.

Sequence Data Types

Sequence data types allow multiple values to be stored in a variable. The five categories of sequence data types are list, tuple, str, set, and dict.

list

Lists are the most commonly used data type in Python by data scientists. A list is an ordered sequence of elements. The elements in the list need not be of the same data type. A list can be declared as items separated by

commas enclosed within square brackets, [ ]. Lists are mutable; i.e., the
value of the elements in the list can be changed. The elements in the list
are indexed starting from zero, and hence any element in the list can be
accessed by its corresponding index, as illustrated in Listing 2-6. The index
should be integers, and using any other data type for index will result in
TypeError. Similarly, trying to access an index outside the range of the list
will result in IndexError.

Listing 2-6. Operations in a List

```
a = [1, 2.5, 5, 3+4j, 3, -2]
print("a is of type",type(a))
"'print the first value in the list"'
print("a[0]=",a[0])
"'print the third value in the list"'
print("a[2]=",a[2])
"' print the values from index 0 to 2"'
print("a[0:3]=",a[0:3])
"'print the values from index 4 till the end of the list"'
print("a[4:]=",a[4:])
"'Change the value at the index 3 to 4"'
a[3]=4
print("a=",a)
"'fractional index leads to TypeError"'
print(a[1.5])
"out of range index leads to IndexError"'
print(a[8])

Output of line 2: a is of type <class 'list'>
Output of line 4: a[0]= 1
Output of line 6: a[2]= 5
Output of line 8: a[0:3]= [1, 2.5, 5]
Output of line 10: a[4:]= [3, -2]
```

```
Output of line 13: a= [1, 2.5, 5, 4, 3, -2]
Otuput of line 15: TypeError: list indices must be integers or
slices, not float
Output of line 17: IndexError: list index out of range
```

Consider two lists stored in the variables a and b, respectively. Table 2-2 shows some additional operations provided by Python that can be performed on the lists a and b. Some of these functions apply to tuples, strings, and sets as well.

Table 2-2. *List Operations in Python*

Function	Description
a+b	Concatenates the two lists a and b
a*n	Repeats the list a by n times where n is an integer
len(a)	Computes the number of elements in list a
a.append()	Adds an element to the end of list a
a.remove()	Removes an item from list a
a.pop()	Removes and returns an element at the given index in list a
a.index()	Returns the index of the first matched item in list a
a.count()	Returns the count of number of items passed as an argument in list a
a.sort()	Sorts items in list a in ascending order
a.reverse()	Reverses the order of items in list a

tuple

A tuple is also an ordered sequence of elements like a list, but the difference is that the tuples are immutable; i.e., the values in a tuple cannot be changed. Trying to change the value of an element in a tuple will result in TypeError. By storing data that doesn't change as tuples, it can be ensured that they remain write-protected. Tuples can be declared as items separated by commas enclosed within parentheses, (). Tuples can also be indexed in the same way as lists, as described in Listing 2-7.

Listing 2-7. Operations in a Tuple

```
a = (1, 3, -2, 4, 6)
print("a is of type",type(a))
print("a[3]=",a[3])
a[2] = 5

Output of line 2: a is of type <class 'tuple'>
Output of line 3: a[3]= 4
Output of line 4: TypeError: 'tuple' object does not support
item assignment
```

str

The str data type represents a string of characters. The string can be declared as characters enclosed within double quotes (" "). Single quotes (' ') can also be used, but since they appear as apostrophes in some words, using double quotes can avoid confusion. The characters in a string are indexed in the same way as list and tuples. The space between two words in a string is also treated as a character. Like tuples, strings are also immutable and described in Listing 2-8.

Listing 2-8. Operations in a String

```
a = "Hello World!"
print("a is of type",type(a))
print("a[3:7]=",a[3:7]
a[2] = "r"
```

```
Output of line 2: a is of type <class 'str'>
Output of line 3: a[3:7]= lo W
Output of line 4: TypeError: 'str' object does not support item
assignment
```

set

A set is an unordered collection of items and hence does not support indexing. A set is defined by values separated by commas inside set braces, {}. A set can be used for removing duplicates from a sequence. Listing 2-9 shows the operations in a set.

Listing 2-9. Operations in a Set

```
a = {1, 2, 3, 2, 4, 1, 3}
print("a is of type",type(a))
print("a=",a)

Output of line 2: a is of type <class 'set'>
Output of line 3: a= {1, 2, 3, 4}
```

Consider two sets stored in variables a and b, respectively. Table 2-3 illustrates the various set operations supported by Python that can be applied on these two sets.

Table 2-3. *Set Operations in Python*

Function	Description
a.union(b)	Returns the union of the two sets a and b in a new set
a.difference(b)	Returns the difference of two sets a and b as a new set
a.intersection(b)	Returns the intersection of the two sets a and b as a new set
a.isdisjoint(b)	Returns True if the two sets a and b have a null intersection
a.issubset(b)	Returns True if a is a subset of b; i.e., all elements of set a are present in set b
a.symmetric_ difference(b)	Returns the symmetric difference between the two sets a and b as a new set

dict

A dict represents the dictionary data type, which is an unordered collection of data represented as key-value pairs. Dictionaries can be defined within set braces, {}, with each item being a pair in the form {key:value}. Dictionaries are optimized for retrieving data where a particular value in the dictionary can be retrieved by using its corresponding key. In other words, the key acts as the index for that value. The key and value can be of any data type. The keys are generally immutable and cannot be duplicated in a dictionary, whereas the values may have duplicate entries. Trying to access a key that is not present in the dictionary will result in KeyError, as described in Listing 2-10.

Listing 2-10. Operations in a Dictionary

```
a = {1: 'Hello', 4: 3.6}
print("a is of type", type(a))
print(a[4])
print(a[2])

Output of line 2: a is of type <class 'dict'>
Output of line 3: 3.6
Output of line 4: KeyError: 2
```

Type Conversion

Type conversion is the process of converting the value of any data type to another data type. The functions provided by Python for type conversion are listed here:

- int(): Changes any data type to the int data type

- float(): Changes any data type to the float data type

- tuple(): Changes any data type to a tuple

- list(): Changes any data type to a list

- set(): Changes any data type to a set

- dict(): Changes any data type to a dictionary

Listing 2-11 illustrates some of these functions.

Listing 2-11. Type Conversion Operations

```
a = 2
print(a)
float(a)
b = [2 , 3, -1, 2, 4, 3]
print(tuple(b))
print(set(b))
```

```
Output of line 2: 2.0
Output of line 4: (2, 3, -1, 2, 4, 3)
Output of line 5: (2, 3, 4, -1)
```

Control Flow Statements

Control flow statements allow for the execution of a statement or a group of statements based on the value of an expression. The control flow statements can be classified into three categories: *sequential control flow statements* that execute the statements in the program in the order they appear, *decision control flow statements* that either execute or skip a block of statements based on whether a condition is True or False, and *loop control flow statements* that allow the execution of a block of statements multiple times until a terminate condition is met.

if Statement

The if control statement in the decision control flow statement category starts with the if keyword, followed by a conditional statement, and ends with a colon. The conditional statement evaluates a Boolean expression and only if the Boolean expression evaluates to True, then the body of statements in the if statement be executed. if block statements start with indentation, and the first statement without indentation marks the end. The syntax for the if statement is as follows, and Listing 2-12 shows how it works:

```
if <expression>:
    <statement(s)>
```

Listing 2-12. if Statement Operations

```
x = 12
y=8
if x > y:
   out = "x is greater than y"
   print(out)

Output: x is greater than y
```

if-else Statement

The if statement can be followed up by an optional else statement. If the Boolean expression corresponding to the conditional statement in the if statement is True, then the statements in the if block are executed, and the statements in the else block are executed if the Boolean expression is False. In other words, the if-else statement provides a two-way decision process. The syntax for the if-else statement is as follows:

```
if <expression>:
    <statement(s)>
else:
    <statement(s)>
```

Listing 2-13 shows the example code for the if-else statement.

Listing 2-13. if-else Statement Operations

```
x = 7
y=9
if x > y:
   out = "x is greater than y"
else:
   out = "x is less than y"
```

```
print(out)
```

```
Output:
x is less than y
```

if...elif...else statement

The if...elif...else statement can provide a multiway decision process. The keyword elif is the short form of else-if. The elif statement can be used along with the if statement if there is a need to select from several possible alternatives. The else statement will come last, acting as the default action. The following is the syntax for the if...elif...else statement, and Listing 2-14 shows the example code:

```
if <expression>:
    <statement(s)>
elif <expression>:
    <statement(s)>
elif <expression>:
    <statement(s)>
...
else:
    <statement(s)>
```

Listing 2-14. if...elif...else Statement Operations

```
x = 4
y=4
if x > y:
   out = "x is greater than y"
elif x<y:
   out = "x is less than y"
```

```
else:
    out = "x is equal to y"
print(out)
```

Output:
```
x is equal to y
```

while loop

The while and for loops are loop control flow statements. In a while loop, the Boolean expression in the conditional statement is evaluated. The block of statements in the while loop is executed only when the Boolean expression is True. Each repetition of the loop block is called an *iteration* of the loop. The Boolean expression in the while statement is checked after each iteration. The execution of the loop is continued until the expression becomes False, and the while loop exits at this point. The syntax for the while loop is as follows, and Listing 2-15 shows how it works:

```
while <expression>:
<statement(s)>
```

Listing 2-15. while Loop Operations

```
x=0
while x < 4:
    print("Hello World!")
    x=x+1
```

Output:
```
Hello World!
Hello World!
Hello World!
Hello World!
```

for loop

The for loop runs with an iteration variable that is incremented with each iteration, and this increment goes on until the variable reaches the end of the sequence on which the loop is operating. In each iteration, the items in the sequence corresponding to the location given by the iteration variable are taken, and the statements in the loop are executed with those items. The syntax for the for loop is as follows:

```
for <iteration_variable> in <sequence>:
    <statement(s)>
```

The range() function is useful in the for loop as it can generate a sequence of numbers that can be iterated using the for loop. The syntax for the range() function is range([start,] stop [,step]) where start indicates the beginning of the sequence (starting from zero if not specified), stop indicates the value up to which the numbers must be generated (not including the number itself), and step indicates the difference between every two consecutive numbers in the generated sequence. The start and step values are optional. The values generated by the range argument should always be integers. Listing 2-16 shows a for loop used to print the elements in a string one by one.

Listing 2-16. for Loop Operations

```
x = "Hello"
for i in x:
    print(i)
```

Output:
```
H
e
l
l
o
```

Listing 2-17 shows how to use the range() function to print a sequence of integers.

Listing 2-17. for Loop Operations with range Function

```
for i in range(4):
    print(i)
```

```
Output:
0
1
2
3
```

Exception Handling

Exceptions are nothing but errors detected during execution. When an exception occurs in a program, the execution is terminated and thereby interrupts the normal flow of the program. By means of exception handling, meaningful information about the error rather than the system-generated message can be provided to the user. Exceptions can be built-in or user-defined. User-defined exceptions are custom exceptions created by the user, which can be done using try...except statements, as shown in Listing 2-18.

Listing 2-18. Exception Handling

```
while True:
try:
    n=int(input("Enter a number"))
print("The number you entered is",n)
    break
```

```
except ValueError:
    print("The number you entered is not
          the correct data type")
    print("Enter a different number")
```

Output:
Enter a number 5
The number you have entered is 5
Enter a number3.6
The number you entered is not the correct data type
Enter a different number

In Listing 2-18, a ValueError exception occurs when a variable receives a value of an inappropriate data type. If no exception occurs, i.e., the number entered as input is an integer, then the except block is skipped, and only the try block is executed. If an exception occurs while entering a number of a different data type, then the rest of the statements in the try block are skipped, the except block is executed, and the program is returned to the try block.

Functions

Functions are fundamental blocks in the Python programming that can be used when a block of statements needs to be executed multiple times within a program. Functions can be created by grouping this block of statements and giving it a name so that the statements can be invoked at any part of the program simply by this name rather than repeating the entire block. Thus, functions can be used to reduce the size of the program by eliminating redundant code. The functions can be either built-in or user-defined.

The Python interpreter has a number of built-in functions some of which we have seen already such as `print()`, `range()`, `len()`, etc. On the other hand, Python enables users to define their own functions and use them as needed. The syntax for function definition is as follows:

```
def function_name(parameter1, .... parameter n):
        statement(s)
```

The function name can have letters, numbers, or an underscore, but it cannot start with a number and should not have the same name as a keyword. Let's consider a simple function that takes a single parameter as input and computes its square; see Listing 2-19.

Listing 2-19. Square Functions

```
def sq(a):
    b = a * a
    print(b)
sq(36)
```

```
Output:1296
```

Let's see a slightly complicated function that computes the binary representation of a given decimal number.

As shown in Listing 2-20, the five lines of code required to compute the binary representation of a decimal number can be replaced by a single line using the user-defined function.

Listing 2-20. Square Functions

```
import math as mt
def dec2bin(a):
    b=' '
    while a!=0:
        b=b+str(a%2)#concatenation operation
```

```
          a=math.floor(a/2)
          return b[:-1]# reverse the string b
    print(int(dec2bin(19)))
```

Output: 10011

Python Libraries for Data Science

The Python community is actively involved in the development of a number of toolboxes intended for various applications. Some of the toolboxes that are used mostly in data science applications are NumPy, SciPy, Pandas, and Scikit-Learn.

NumPy and SciPy for Scientific Computation

NumPy is a scientific computation package available with Python. NumPy provides support for multidimensional arrays, linear algebra functions, and matrices. NumPy array representations provide an effective data structure for data scientists. A NumPy array is called an *ndarray*, and it can be created using the array() function. Listing 2-21 illustrates how to create 1D and 2D arrays and how to index their elements.

Listing 2-21. Array Using NumPy

```
'''import the NumPy library'''
import numpy as np
'''creates an 1D array'''
a=np.array([1,2,3,4])
'''print the data type of variable a'''
print(type(a))
'''creates a 2D array'''
a=np.array([[1, 2, 3, 4], [5, 6, 7, 8]])
```

```
print(a)
'''print the dimension of the array'''
print(a.ndim)
'''print the number of rows and columns in the array'''
print(a.shape)
'''print the third element in the first row'''
print(a[0,2])
'''print the sliced matrix as per given index'''
print(a[0:2,1:3])
a=np.array([1, 2, 3, 4, 5, 6, 7, 8, 9])
'''reshape the 1 x 9 array into a 3 x 3 array'''
b=a.reshape(3,3))
print(b)
```

```
Output of line 6: <class 'numpy.ndarray'>
Output of line 9:
[[1 2 3 4]
 [5 6 7 8]]
Output of line 11: 2
Output of line 13: (2, 4)
Output of line 15:3
Output of line 17
[[2 3]
 [6 7]]
Output of line 21:
[[1 2 3]
 [4 5 6]
 [7 8 9]]
```

The sum of elements in an array of any dimension can be computed using sum(). The sum can be computed either for the entire elements in the array or along one of the dimensions as illustrated in Listing 2-22 for the array b created earlier.

Listing 2-22. Array Using NumPy

```
'''print the sum of elements in array b'''
print(b.sum())
'''print the sum of elements along each column'''
print(b.sum(axis=0))
'''print the sum of elements along each row'''
print(b.sum(axis=1))

Output:
Output of line 2: 45
Output of line 4: array([12,15,18])
Output of line 6: array([6, 15, 18])
```

Another important operation with respect to arrays is the flattening of multidimensional arrays. This process is more common in many of the machine learning–based applications, and it can be done by using the flatten() function, as illustrated here:

```
b.flatten()
Output:
        array([1, 2, 3, 4, 5, 6, 7, 8, 9]
```

The flatten() function converts an array of any dimension into a single-dimensional array. This can be achieved using reshape() as well, but unlike the flatten() function, the size of the single-dimensional array has to be specified in that case. Table 2-4 describes some other array operations that may come in handy while working with data analysis applications.

Table 2-4. *NumPy Functions for Data Analysis*

Syntax	Description
np.ones()	Creates an array of ones in the dimension specified within the parentheses.
np.zeros()	Creates an array of zeros in the dimension specified within the parentheses.
np.flip(a,axis)	Reverses the array a along the given axis. If axis is not specified, the array is reversed along both dimensions.
np.concatenate(a,b,axis)	Concatenates two arrays a and b along the specified axis (=0 or 1 corresponding to vertical and horizontal direction).
np.split(a,n)	Splits the array a into n number of smaller arrays. Here n can be any positive integer.
np.where(a==n)	Gives the index values of the number n present in an array a.
np.sort(a,axis)	Sorts the numbers in an array a along the given axis.
np.random.randint(n,size)	Generates an array of the given size using integers ranging from 0 to the number n.

The SciPy ecosystem is a collection of open source software for scientific computation built on the NumPy extension of Python. It provides high-level commands for manipulating and visualizing data. Two major components of this ecosystem are the SciPy library, which is a collection of numerical algorithms and domain-specific toolboxes, and Matplotlib, which is a plotting package that provides 2D and 3D plotting. The following syntax can be used to import and use any function from a SciPy module in your code:

```
from scipy import some_module
some_module.some_function()
```

As per the official SciPy documentation, the library is organized into different subtypes covering different domains, as summarized in Table 2-5.

Table 2-5. *Subpackages in SciPY*

Subpackage	Description
cluster	Clustering algorithms
constants	Physical and mathematical constants
fftpack	Fast Fourier Transform routines
integrate	Integration and ordinary differential equation solvers
interpolate	Interpolation and smoothing splines
io	Input and output
linalg	Linear algebra
ndimage	N-dimensional image processing
odr	Orthogonal distance regression
optimize	Optimization and root-finding routines
signal	Signal processing
sparse	Sparse matrices and associated routines
spatial	Spatial data structures and algorithms
special	Special functions
stats	Statistical distributions and functions

Scikit-Learn for Machine Learning

Scikit-Learn is an open source machine learning library for Python programming that features various classification, regression, and clustering algorithms. It is designed to interoperate with other Python libraries like NumPy and SciPy.

Pandas for Data Analysis

Pandas is a fast and powerful open source library for data analysis and manipulation written for Python programming. It has a fast and efficient DataFrame object for data manipulation with integrated indexing. It has tools for reading and writing data between in-memory data structures and different file formats such as CSV, Microsoft Excel, etc. Consider a CSV file called data.csv containing the grades of three students in three subjects, as shown in Figure 2-5. Listing 2-23 shows the procedure for reading and accessing this data using Pandas.

Roll No	Science	Maths	English
RN001	70	76	85
RN002	86	98	88
RN003	76	65	74

Figure 2-5. *CSV file with grade data of students*

Listing 2-23. Data Modification Using Pandas Functions

```
import pandas as pd
'''reads the file data.csv with read_csv package and the
header=None option allows pandas to assign default names to the
colums
Consider the data in the above table is typed in a excel sheet and
saved as csv file in the following path C:\Python_book\data.csv
```

```
'''
d = pd.read_csv("C:\Python_book\data.csv",header=None)
print(type(d))
print(d)
"'print the element common to row1-column2"'
print(d.loc[1,2])
"'print the elements common to rows 1,2 and
  columns 1,2"'
d.loc[1:2, 1:2]

Output of line 4:
<class 'pandas.core.frame.DataFrame'>
Output of line 5:
        0          1       2         3
0   Roll No    Science  Maths   English
1    RN001        70      76        85
2    RN002        86      98        88
3    RN003        76      65        74
Output of line 7: 76
Output of line 9:
     1      2
1   70     76
2   86     98
```

Similarly, there are other read functions such as read_excel, read_sql, read_html, etc., to read files in other formats, and every one of these read functions comes with their corresponding write functions like to_csv, to_excel, to_sql, to_html, etc., that allows you to write the Pandas dataframe to different formats.

Most of the real-time data gathered from sensors is in the form of time-series data, which is a series of data indexed in time order. Let's consider a dataset that consists of the minimum daily temperatures in degrees Celsius over 10 years (1981 to 1990) in Melbourne, Australia. The source of the data is the Australian Bureau of Meteorology. Even though this is also a CSV file, it is time-series data unlike the DataFrame in the previous illustration. Listing 2-24 shows the different ways to explore the time-series data.

Listing 2-24. Data Modification in Pandas

```
Series=pd.read_csv('daily-min-
            temperatures.csv',header=0, index_col=0)
"'prints first 5 data from the top of the series"'
print(series.head(5))
"'prints the number of entries in the series"'
print(series.size)
print(series.describe())
"'describe() function creates 7 descriptive   statistics of the
time series data including mean, standard deviation, median,
minimum, and maximum of the observations"'

    Output of line 3:
  Date                    Temp
1981-01-01              20.7
1981-01-02              17.9
1981-01-03              18.8
1981-01-04              14.6
1981-01-05              15.8
Output of line 5: 3650
Output of line 6:
```

```
             Temp
count   3650.000000
mean      11.177753
std        4.071837
min        0.000000
25%        8.300000
50%       11.000000
75%       14.000000
max       26.300000
```

TensorFlow for Machine Learning

TensorFlow is an end-to-end open source platform for machine learning created by the Google Brain team. TensorFlow has a slew of machine learning models and algorithms. It uses Python to provide a front-end API for building applications with the framework. Keras is a high-level neural network API that runs on top of TensorFlow. Keras allows for easy and fast prototyping and supports both convolutional networks and recurrent neural networks.

CHAPTER 3

Introduction to the Raspberry Pi

The Raspberry Pi, or simply the Pi, is a series of small, low-cost, single-board computers invented by the Raspberry Pi Foundation in the United Kingdom to promote basic computer science and electronics among students around the world. Students and tech enthusiasts use the Raspberry Pi to learn programming concepts, build hardware projects and robots, and make artificial intelligence projects. It is also used in industrial applications.

What Can You Do with the Raspberry Pi?

A Raspberry Pi board can do pretty much everything a desktop computer can do: surf the Internet, watch high-definition videos, listen to music, view and edit pictures, perform word processing, make spreadsheets and presentations, write and compile code, participate in video conferencing, and even play games.

© K. Mohaideen Abdul Kadhar and G. Anand 2021
K. M. Abdul Kadhar and G. Anand, *Data Science with Raspberry Pi*,
https://doi.org/10.1007/978-1-4842-6825-4_3

Physical Computing with the Raspberry Pi

The Raspberry Pi can also be used to interact with the physical world. This is done with the general-purpose input/output (GPIO) pins on the Raspberry Pi board. This makes the Raspberry Pi powerful as it can be interfaced with sensors and other electric and electronic components such as LEDs, servo and stepper motors, relays, etc.

How to Program the Raspberry Pi?

The Raspberry Pi comes with two pre-installed languages (Scratch and Python), but it also supports other languages. Scratch is a visual programming language for children, whereas Python is a high-level general-purpose programming language; both languages are easy to learn. If you learn to program in Python, then you can do everything that's possible with the Raspberry Pi.

Raspberry Pi Hardware

The Raspberry Pi Foundation released the first Raspberry Pi, the Raspberry Pi model B, in 2012. A number of improved versions were released after that, and we will look at all those versions later. The latest version is the Raspberry Pi 4 model B, released in June 2019. Figure 3-1 shows the top view of a Raspberry Pi board with its many I/O ports. Let's take a look at its hardware specifications and other features.

Figure 3-1. *Raspberry Pi hardware*

System on a Chip

The *system on a chip* (SoC), shown in Figure 3-2, is the brain of the Raspberry Pi. This small chip consists of many important parts: the central processing unit (CPU), the graphics processing unit (GPU), and the digital signal processor.

Figure 3-2. *System on a chip*

The Raspberry Pi 4 model B has the powerful Broadcom BCM2711 (1.5 GHz 64-bit quad-core) SoC. The Pi's CPU performs operations such as basic arithmetic, logic, controlling, and input/output, while the Pi's GPU is used for handling multimedia tasks such as digital image processing, drawing 3D graphics, and playing games.

Raspberry Pi RAM

Random access memory (RAM) is the black rectangle located next to the SoC in the Raspberry Pi 4 model B, as shown in Figure 3-3. In previous versions of the Raspberry Pi, the RAM was packed inside the SoC. The Pi 4 offers three choices of LPDDR4 RAM: 1GB, 2GB, and 4GB.

Figure 3-3. *Raspberry Pi RAM*

RAM stores the short-term data used by the applications, and this data will be deleted when the Raspberry Pi is turned off. The RAM is shared by both the central processing unit and the graphics processing unit.

Connectivity

The Raspberry Pi 4 model B has onboard Wi-Fi, Bluetooth and Gigabit Ethernet. These features come in handy for accessing the Raspberry Pi remotely, making it a desirable choice of hardware for Internet of Things (IoT) projects. This also frees up the USB ports and GPIO pins for connecting external Wi-Fi and Bluetooth modules.

Setting Up the Raspberry Pi

This section explains how to set up the Raspberry Pi.

microSD Memory Card

The Raspberry Pi, unlike desktops and laptops, uses a microSD memory card for storing the files, applications, and even the operating system. microSD memory cards are small compared to hard disks and are easy to use. A minimum of 8GB of memory is required by the Pi. A 16GB or 32GB microSD memory card is recommended for data science projects. Class 10 ultra-high-speed (UHS) memory cards are recommended for faster reading/writing of data.

Installing the OS

Raspbian is the official and most commonly used operating system for the Raspberry Pi released by the Raspberry Pi Foundation. It can be easily installed on the microSD card using Raspberry Pi Imager software, as shown in Figure 3-4. The Raspberry Pi also supports other operating systems such as Ubuntu and Windows 10 IOT Core.

Figure 3-4. Interface of the Raspberry Pi Imager software

Follow these instructions to install the Raspbian OS in your Raspberry Pi:

1. Visit the Downloads page of the Raspberry Pi website and download the Raspberry Pi Imager software on your operating system.

2. Once the download is completed, launch the installer by clicking it.

3. Insert the microSD memory card into your computer. Make sure to back up any important data you have in it, as anything stored in the card will be formatted.

4. Select the Raspbian or other desired operating
    system that you want to install and also the microSD
    card you would like to install it on.

5. Finally, click the Write button and wait for the
    operation to complete.

Inserting the microSD Memory Card

The thin metal slot on the underside of the Raspberry Pi, as shown in
Figure 3-5, is the microSD memory card slot. Once the operating system is
installed on the microSD memory card, insert it in the memory card slot of
the Raspberry Pi.

Figure 3-5. *MicroSD card slot*

As the operating system is stored along with the other files on the
microSD memory card, it makes the Pi's memory portable. The microSD
memory card can be inserted in a new Raspberry Pi, and it will work like a
charm.

Connecting a Keyboard and Mouse

Figure 3-6 shows the USB ports of a Raspberry Pi pin. The Raspberry Pi 4 model B has two USB 2.0 ports (black) and two Universal Serial Bus (USB) 3.0 ports (blue). USB can be used to connect a keyboard, mouse, webcam, and other USB peripherals. USB 3.0 ports are about 10 times faster than the USB 2.0 ports. Normally, peripherals like keyboard and mouse are connected to the USB 2.0 ports, leaving the faster USB 3.0 ports for devices such as hard disk and webcam.

Figure 3-6. *USB ports*

If you have a wireless keyboard and mouse instead of a wired combination, they can be connected to the Raspberry Pi by connecting the USB dongle in one of the two black ports. This also frees up one of the USB ports, which can be used to connect other devices.

Connecting a Monitor

The Raspberry Pi can be connected to a monitor through the micro-HDMI port shown in Figure 3-7. HDMI stands for High-Definition Multimedia Interface, and the Raspberry Pi provides combined audio and video output from this port. The Raspberry Pi model 4 comes with two micro-HDMI ports with 4K support, which means you can connect two 4K monitors to the Raspberry Pi at the same time.

Figure 3-7. *HDMI ports*

If your TV or monitor supports HDMI input, then you will need a micro HDMI-to-HDMI cable to connect the Raspberry Pi to your TV or monitor. Older versions of the Raspberry Pi come with a single HDMI port. If your TV or monitor has a VGA input, then you will need to use a micro HDMI-to-VGA adapter to connect it to the Raspberry Pi. Similarly, you can use a HDMI-to-DVI cable for monitors with DVI input.

Powering the Raspberry Pi

The Raspberry Pi 4 B needs to be powered through a 5.1V DC USB-C type connector, as shown in Figure 3-8, with a minimum current input of 3A. It can also be powered via the GPIO header. The USB-C type power port is located near a corner of the Raspberry Pi. None of the Raspberry Pi models has an on/off switch; once you connect the Raspberry Pi to the power supply, it turns on.

Figure 3-8. *USB-C type connector*

Supplying the incorrect voltage or insufficient current can cause damages to the Raspberry Pi; hence, it is recommended to use the official Raspberry Pi power supply.

Raspberry Pi Enclosure

The Raspberry Pi needs to be enclosed in a case to prevent the bare connections and GPIO headers. A variety of enclosure cases are available for the Raspberry Pi, or you can make your own case, but it is recommended to use the official cases released by the Raspberry Pi Foundation. Cases with cooling fans are also available. They can be used to prevent the Pi from overheating while running heavy-duty applications.

Raspberry Pi Versions

This section explains the different versions.

Raspberry Pi 1

The Raspberry Pi B was the first model launched by the Raspberry Pi Foundation in 2012, followed by the Pi A in 2013. They had 26 GPIO pins, a 700MHz processor, and 256MB/512MB RAM, and they didn't have any built-in Wi-Fi or Bluetooth. In 2014, the compact Pi A+ and improved B+ models were released with 40 GPIO pins.

Raspberry Pi 2

The Raspberry Pi 2 was released in 2015 with an improved 900MHz quad-core processor and 1GB RAM. This model had 40 GPIO pins and did not have built-in Wi-Fi or Bluetooth. It had four USB 2.0 ports, an Ethernet port, and an HDMI port.

Raspberry Pi 3

In 2016, the Raspberry Pi 3 was released. It had a 1.2GHz quad-core processor with 1GB RAM. This model had 40 GPIO pins, and this was the first Raspberry Pi model to have built-in Wi-Fi and Bluetooth. Similar to the Raspberry Pi 2, it had four USB 2.0 ports, an Ethernet port, and an HDMI port. Later in 2018, the compact Pi 3 A+ and improved Pi 3 B+ models were launched.

Raspberry Pi Zero (W/WH)

In 2015, a small-sized, low-cost Raspberry Pi Zero with fewer GPIO pins was launched. The Pi Zero W was released in 2017 with built-in Wi-Fi and Bluetooth. This was followed by the Pi Zero WH that came with pre-soldered GPIO headers.

Raspberry Pi 4

The Raspberry Pi 4 model B was released in 2019 and had the powerful 1.5GHz quad-core processor and 1GB/2GB/4GB RAM options. This was the first model to come with dual 4K display output, USB-C type power input, and two USB 3.0 ports.

Recommended Raspberry Pi Version

There are different versions of Raspberry Pi available, but the Raspberry Pi 4 is recommended for data science projects as it is more powerful than the other versions and also comes with RAM options up to 4GB.

The Raspberry Pi Zero WH is the smallest variant of the Raspberry Pi available, and it is recommended when the size of the single-board computer needs to be small. But it comes with a comparatively slower processor, less RAM, and fewer GPIO pins.

Interfacing the Raspberry Pi with Sensors

This section highlights how to interface the Raspberry Pi with sensors.

GPIO Pins

The GPIO pins shown in Figure 3-9 are one of the most powerful features of the Raspberry Pi. The GPIO pins are the row of little pins along the edge of the board. All Raspberry Pi versions released recently have a 40-pin GPIO header. These pins are the connections between the Raspberry Pi and the real world. GPIO pins can be designated as input or output in software and can be used for a variety of purposes like turning on/off LEDs, controlling servo motors, and getting data from sensors. They can be programmed in Python or any other language such as Scratch or C/C++.

Pin Number

	Pin	Pin	
3V3	1	2	5V
GPIO 2	3	4	5V
GPIO 3	5	6	GND
GPIO 4	7	8	GPIO 14
GND	9	10	GPIO 15
GPIO 17	11	12	GPIO 18
GPIO 27	13	14	GND
GPIO 22	15	16	GPIO 23
3V3	17	18	GPIO 24
GPIO 10	19	20	GND
GPIO 9	21	22	GPIO 25
GPIO 11	23	24	GPIO 8
GND	25	26	GPIO 7
DNC	27	28	DNC
GPIO 5	29	30	GND
GPIO 6	31	32	GPIO 12
GPIO 13	33	34	GND
GPIO 19	35	36	GPIO 16
GPIO 26	37	38	GPIO 20
GND	39	40	GPIO 21

Figure 3-9. Raspberry Pi GPIO pins

GPIO Pinout

Before making any connections to the Raspberry Pi GPIO pins, we need
to know the GPIO pinout reference. Pinout configurations are not printed
on the Raspberry Pi, but we can get the pinout reference of any Raspberry

Pi by opening the terminal window and typing the command `pinout`. This tool is given by the `gpiozero` library, which is pre-installed on the Raspbian OS.

GPIO Outputs

The Raspberry Pi has two 5V pins and two 3V3 pins; it also has eight ground pins (0V), which cannot be configured. The remaining 28 pins are all general-purpose 3V3 pins. The outputs of these pins are set to 3V3 or can receive inputs up to 3V3. A GPIO pin designated as an output pin can be set to high (3V3) or low (0V).

Controlling GPIO Output with Python

GPIO pins can be easily controlled with Python using the `gpiozero` library. Let's see a simple Python example of how to turn on/off LEDs connected to GPIO pins. LEDs always need to be connected to the GPIO pins through a resistor. Resistors will ensure that only a small current will flow in the circuit; hence, the Raspberry Pi or the LED will be protected from damage.

We will connect an LED to GPIO pin 17 through a 330Ω resistor, as shown in Figure 3-10. Now, the LED can be made to continuously turn on and off using the Python code given in Listing 3-1. The `led.on()` function turns on the LED, and the `led.off()` function turns off the LED.

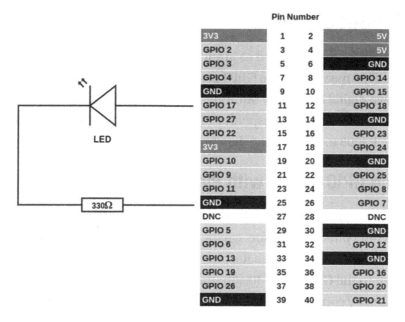

Figure 3-10.   *Connecting LED to GPIO pins*

Listing 3-1.   LED Function Using GPIO

```
from gpiozero import LED
from time import sleep
led = LED(17)
while True:
      led.on()
      sleep(1)
      led.off()
      sleep(1)
```

GPIO Input Signals

GPIO pins that are designated as input pins can be read as high (3V3) or low (0V). This means that the GPIO pins do not support analog input and can receive digital input only. Although there is no hardware for an analog-to-digital converter in the Raspberry Pi, we can use an external ADC such as the MCP3008 to read analog data from sensors.

Reading GPIO Inputs with Python

Sensors can be easily interfaced with the Raspberry Pi by connecting them to GPIO pins. The sensors can be powered by connecting the VCC of the sensor to 3.3V/5V of the Raspberry Pi and connecting the GND of the sensor to the GND of the Raspberry Pi. Digital output from the sensor can be directly connected to the GPIO pins and read. But while reading an analog output, an analog-to-digital converter required to interface a analog sensor with Raspberry Pi.

Digital Signals from Sensors

The Raspberry Pi considers any input below 1.8V as low (0) and anything above 1.8V as high (1), as shown in Figure 3-11. Digital output data from any sensor can be easily read using the `InputDevice.value` function. This function returns the current state of the given GPIO pin.

Figure 3-11. *Low and high inputs*

The code in the Listing 3-2 prints the state of GPIO pin 17 every second.

Listing 3-2. State of GPIO

```
from gpiozero import InputDevice
from time import sleep
sensor = InputDevice(17, pull_up=True)
while True:
        print(sensor.value)
        sleep(1)
```

Analog Signals from Sensors

Figure 3-12 illustrates an analog signal. To read analog signals from sensors or some other devices, we should use an analog-to-digital converter such as MCP3008 for the Raspberry Pi. An ADC converts the analog signals into digital signals. The Serial Peripheral Interface (SPI) protocol is used to communicate the output from the ADC to the Raspberry Pi.

Figure 3-12. *Analog signal*

To enable SPI communication, open the Raspberry Pi configuration from the main menu and enable SPI on the Interfaces tab. MCP3008 is a 10-bit ADC and has eight input channels (0–7). Let's connect an analog input to the first channel (0) of the MCP3008 and the other pins of the MCP3008, as shown in Figure 3-13.

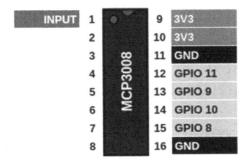

Figure 3-13. *10-bit ADC MCP3008*

The code in Listing 3-3 prints the analog value of the sensor connected to the first channel (0) of MCP3008 every second. Since MCP3008 is a 10-bit ADC, the output value ranges from 0 to 1023.

Listing 3-3. Implement the MCP3008

```
from gpiozero import MCP3008
from time import sleep
sensor = MCP3008(0)
while True:
        print(sensor.value)
        sleep(1)
```

Interfacing a Ultrasonic Sensor with the Raspberry Pi

Ultrasonic sensors are used to measure the distance of objects by finding the time of the sound wave. The HC-SR04 ultrasonic sensor can be used to measure the distance from 2cm to 400cm with 3mm accuracy. Ultrasonic sensors work by sending out a sound wave at a frequency of 40kHz, which is above the range of human hearing and travels through the air. If there is an obstacle or object, the sound wave will bounce back to the sensor.

The distance of the object can be calculated by multiplying half of the travel time and the speed of sound. Figure 3-14 shows the ultrasonic sensor and its pins where the VCC pin needs to be connected to the positive terminal of the Raspberry Pi, the GND pin can be connected to a GND pin of the Raspberry Pi, the Trig pin is used to trigger the ultrasonic sound pulses, and the Echo pin produces a pulse when the reflected sound wave is received.

Figure 3-14.   *Ultrasonic sensor pin*

Connect the ultrasonic distance sensor to the Raspberry Pi, as shown in Figure 3-15.

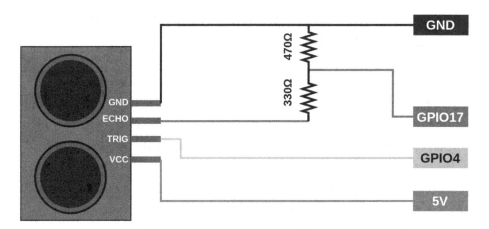

Figure 3-15.   *Ultrasonic sensor with the Raspberry Pi GPIO pin*

The gpiozero library has an object called DistanceSensor that can be used to measure distance using the ultrasonic sensor in Python. The distance function returns the distance measure by the ultrasonic distance senor in meters. Let's multiply the value by 100 to convert it into centimeters. The code in Listing 3-4 continuously prints the distance measure by the ultrasonic distance sensor in centimeters every second.

Listing 3-4. Code for calculting distance measured by the Ultrasonic Sensor

```
from gpiozero import DistanceSensor
from time import sleep

sensor = DistanceSensor(echo=17, trigger=4)

while True:
    print(sensor.distance * 100)
    sleep(1)
```

When the code is running, move the position of the objects placed in front of the ultrasonic sensor to get different values.

Interfacing the Temperature and Humidity Sensor with the Raspberry Pi

As the name suggests, these sensors can be used to measure the temperature and humidity. They consist of a capacitive humidity sensing element and a thermistor for sensing temperature. The temperature and humidity sensor has a dedicated resistive-type humidity measurement component, called the *negative temperature coefficient* (NTC) temperature measurement component, and an 8-bit microcontroller to output the values of temperature and humidity as serial data. A single-bus data format is used for the communication and synchronization between the Raspberry Pi and the DHT11 sensor.

DHT 11 and DHT 22 are the generally used temperature and humidity sensors. Figure 3-16 shows the temperature and humidity sensor (THD) and Figure 3-17 explains the interfacing of THD with Raspberry Pi where the VCC pin needs to be connected to the positive terminal of the Raspberry Pi, where the GND pin can be connected to a GND of the Raspberry Pi, and where the Signal/Data pin is used for serial communication and needs to connect to a GPIO pin.

Figure 3-16. *Temperature and humidity sensor*

Connect the DHT 11/22 sensor module to the Raspberry Pi, as shown in Figure 3-17.

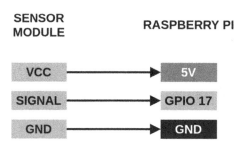

Figure 3-17. *Temperature and humidity sensor with the Raspberry Pi GPIO pin*

Let's use the Adafruit_DHT library to get the temperature and humidity values from the sensor. The code in Listing 3-5 continuously prints the temperature in Celsius and the humidity percentage.

Listing 3-5. Code for Temperature and Humidity Sensor

```
import Adafruit_DHT
import time

DHT_SENSOR = Adafruit_DHT.DHT11
DHT_PIN = 17

while True:
    humidity, temperature =
        Adafruit_DHT.read(DHT_SENSOR, DHT_PIN)
    if humidity is not None and temperature is not None:
        print("Temperature="{0:0.1f}C)
      humidity={1:0.1f}%".format(temperature, humidity))
    else:
        print("Sensor not connected.");
    time.sleep(3);
```

The Adafruit module can be installed in the Raspberry Pi using the following code.

For Python 2:

```
sudo pip install Adafruit_DHT
```

For Python 3:

```
sudo pip3 install Adafruit_DHT
```

Interfacing the Soil Moisture Sensor with the Raspberry Pi

Soil moisture sensors are used to detect the moisture present in soil. A soil moisture sensor consists of two probes that are used to measure the amount of moisture present in the soil. This sensor uses capacitance to measure the dielectric permittivity of the soil, which is a function of the moisture content of the soil. The sensor is equipped with both analog and digital output, so it can be used in both analog and digital modes. But, let's take the analog signal from the sensor and read it using Python. Figure 3-18 shows the soil moisture sensor. Here, the VCC pin needs to be connected to the positive terminal of the Raspberry Pi, the analog output (AO) creates a voltage proportional to the dielectric permittivity and therefore the water content of the soil, and the digital output (DO) creates a pulse when the soil moisture is higher than the threshold value. The threshold value is set using the potentiometer in the sensor module, and the GND pin can be connected to a GND of the Raspberry Pi.

Figure 3-18. *Soil moisture sensor*

Connect the soil moisture sensor module to the Raspberry Pi through an MCP3008 ADC, as shown in Figure 3-19.

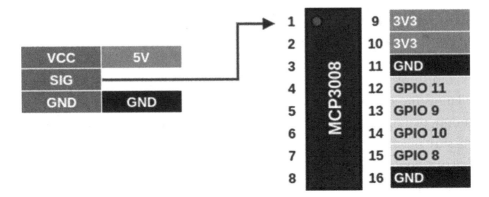

Figure 3-19. *Temperature and humidity sensor with the Raspberry Pi GPIO pin*

Let's use the MCP3008 module from the gpiozero library to get the values from the MCP3008. The code in Listing 3-6 continuously prints the analog value of the soil moisture sensor every second.

Listing 3-6. Code for interfacing soil moisture sensor

```
from gpiozero import MCP3008
from time import sleep

soil_sensor = MCP3008(0)

while True:
    print(soil_sensor.value)
    sleep(1)
```

Interfacing Cameras with the Raspberry Pi

Cameras are optical instruments used to record images using an image sensor. An image sensor detects and conveys information used to make an image. Cameras can be easily interfaced with the Raspberry Pi to get image or video data. There are two options available to interface cameras with the Raspberry Pi.

Method 1: The first method is to connect a USB web camera to the Raspberry Pi using the USB ports. Figure 3-20 shows a USB web camera. Once the USB web camera is connected properly, it can be accessed in Python using the OpenCV library. OpenCV is a Python library for image processing and real-time computer vision. The code in Listing 3-7 can be used for connecting the USB web camera to the Raspberry Pi.

Figure 3-20. *USB web camera*

Listing 3-7. Code for Connecting USB Web Cameras with the Raspberry Pi

```
import cv2

videoCaptureObject = cv2.VideoCapture(0)
result = True

while(result):
    ret,frame = videoCaptureObject.read()
    cv2.imwrite("/home/pi/Desktop/webcam_image.jpg ",frame)
    result = False

videoCaptureObject.release()
cv2.destroyAllWindows()
```

Method 2: Another method is to interface a Raspberry Pi camera module via the Camera Serial Interface (CSI) port. Figure 3-21 shows the Raspberry Pi camera. There are two Raspberry Pi camera modules

73

available: a standard module and a NoIR camera module for taking pictures in the dark. To enable the Raspberry Pi camera, open the Raspberry Pi configuration from the main menu and enable Camera on the Interfaces tab.

Figure 3-21.   *Raspberry Pi camera with CSI*

The code in Listing 3-8 takes a picture from the Raspberry Pi camera module and stores the image in the specified location.

Listing 3-8.   Code for Connecting Raspberry Pi Camera with the Raspberry Pi

```
from picamera import PiCamera
from time import sleep

camera = PiCamera()

camera.start_preview()
sleep(5)
camera.capture('/home/pi/Desktop/cammodule_img.jpg')
camera.stop_preview()
```

Raspberry Pi as an Edge Device

Computing done at or near the source of data is known as *edge computing*. Edge computing is preferred over cloud computing in areas that require instant or real-time computing, as well as in remote locations that cannot be connected to a centralized cloud or have limited connectivity. The most significant advantage of edge computing is its capacity to reduce latency as the data gathered by the sensors is processed in edge devices and doesn't need to travel far to the data centers. See Figure 3-22.

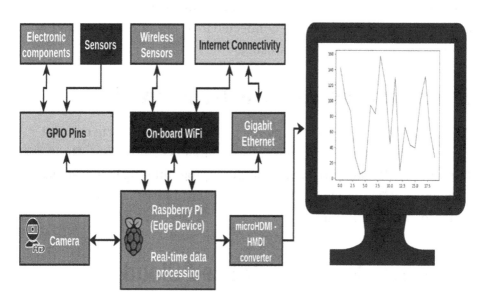

Figure 3-22. *Raspberry Pi as edge device*

Edge Computing in Self-Driving Cars

Self-driving cars will rely on edge computing as every millisecond is very crucial while driving on the road. The large amount of data collected from their sensors and cameras can't be sent to the cloud for analysis as this would take a considerable amount of time and also need an uninterrupted network. So, edge computing is preferred for these kind of applications due to its faster speed and high reliability.

What Is an Edge Device?

Edge computing is done in edge devices. Edge devices are capable of gathering, storing, and processing data in real time. As a result, the edge devices provide faster response and have better reliability. Sensors and other devices are connected to the edge device via wired cables or wireless connectivity such as Wi-Fi or Bluetooth, as shown in Figure 3-22. Sometimes the edge devices are connected to a centralized cloud for big data processing and data warehousing.

Edge Computing with the Raspberry Pi

The Raspberry Pi has good computing power and the ability to connect to sensors and devices through wired and wireless connections. The Raspberry Pi also supports many computer programming languages such as Python, C/C++, and Java. This makes the Raspberry Pi an excellent choice for edge computing.

Raspberry Pi as a Localized Cloud

In this chapter, we'll discuss using the Raspberry Pi as a localized cloud.

Cloud Computing

Cloud computing is the practice of using a network of remote servers hosted on the Internet to store, manage, and process data. These remote servers are called *cloud servers* and are located in data centers all over the world. Accessing data from these kind of servers requires strong Internet connectivity.

Raspberry Pi as Localized Cloud

Nowadays, IoT devices generate huge volumes of data at high speed. Often this data requires real-time processing to make quick decisions, and this can be supported by a localized cloud. Also, some of the IoT sensor networks are deployed at remote areas with sparse Internet connectivity, which challenges the concept of a localized cloud. The Raspberry Pi can be made as a localized cloud to support real-time data processing closer to the IoT networks. It needs to be connected to a network via Ethernet or Wi-Fi. The Raspberry Pi as a localized cloud can be used to store and process data collected from sensors or from other devices such as computers and mobile phones, as illustrated in Figure 3-23.

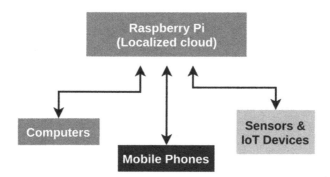

Figure 3-23. *Raspberry Pi as a localized cloud*

Connecting an External Hard Drive

External hard disk drives can be connected to the Raspberry Pi to increase its storage capacity. These HDDs need to be powered externally using a power supply. If there is no power supply, they can be connected via a powered USB hub. This enhanced storage can allow the Raspberry Pi to collect and process large amounts of real-time data from IoT networks.

Connecting USB Accelerator

Coral USB Accelerator is a super-fast development board for deep learning practitioners to deploy their models without the need for the Internet, thereby enabling edge computing. It brings a machine learning interface to the Raspberry Pi. It consists of an edge TPU coprocessor, which is capable of performing 4 trillion operations (tera-operations) per second (TOPS). This makes running ML models in real time possible. For example, the device can help the Raspberry Pi run MobileNet v2 models at 400 FPS.

CHAPTER 4

Sensors and Signals

This chapter covers sensors and signals.

Signals

Generally, signals represent some information with respect to time or space. For example, a variation of a car's speed with respect to time is a kind of signal. The information can be transferred in the form of signals. In electrical engineering, a signal is a function that carries information with respect to time or space. The electrical equipment exhibits the signals in the form of voltage, current, or electromagnetic waves. As per the *IEEE Transactions on Signal Processing*, a signal can be audio, video, speech, image, sonar, radar-related, and so on [1]. Also, mathematically speaking, a signal is a function of one or more independent variables. Independent variables are just variables that aren't changed by the other variables you are trying to measure. For example, consider the temperature variation with respect to time. Here, time is the independent variable, because the time isn't changed due to the variations in the temperature.

This chapter discusses how to acquire information from a real-time environment using sensors with Raspberry Pi and then convert that information in to structured data. The sensor output is in the form of an

© K. Mohaideen Abdul Kadhar and G. Anand 2021
K. M. Abdul Kadhar and G. Anand, *Data Science with Raspberry Pi*,
https://doi.org/10.1007/978-1-4842-6825-4_4

electrical signal. This chapter first describes about signal and its various types. There are many classifications of signals of which we concentrate on describing the following electrical signals:

- Analog and digital signals

- Continuous-time and discrete-time signals

- Deterministic and nondeterministic signals

- One-dimensional signals, two-dimensional signals, multidimensional signals

Analog and Digital Signals

An *analog signal* represents the instantaneous values of a physical quantity that varies continuously with respect to an independent variable (i.e., time). Simply speaking, analog signals are continuous in time and amplitude. The physical quantity may be temperature, pressure, speed, etc. Sensors can convert the variation of physical quantity in to electrical signals like voltage or current. In this way, real-time environment data can be collected in the form of electrical signals using sensors.

A *digital signal* is a signal that is used to represent data as a sequence of discrete values. The independent variable (i.e., time) is discrete and has quantized amplitude. Digital signals can be obtained by applying sampling and quantization on analog signals. At any given time the digital signal can take on only one of a finite number of values.

Continuous-Time and Discrete-Time Signals

A *continuous time signal* or *continuous signal* is a signal defined over a continuum of its domain, which is often time. Any analog signal is continuous by nature.

A *discrete-time signal* or *discrete signal* is a signal whose independent variable (time) has only discrete values. It is a time series consisting of a sequence of quantities. Discrete-time signals, used in digital signal processing, can be obtained by sampling and quantization of continuous signals.

Deterministic and Nondeterministic Signals

A *deterministic signal* is a signal with no uncertainty with respect to its value at any instant in time. In other words, a signal that can be defined exactly using a mathematical formula is a deterministic signal.

A *nondeterministic signal* or *random signal* is a signal that has uncertainty with respect to its value at some instant in time. This signal is also called a *random signal* due to its random nature, and the signal cannot be described by a mathematical equation.

One-Dimensional, Two-Dimensional, and Multidimensional Signals

A *one-dimensional signal* is a function of only one independent variable. Voice signal is a good example of one-dimensional signal, because the amplitude of voice depends on only one independent variable (i.e., time).

Similarly, if the signal is a function of two dependent variables, the signal is called a *two-dimensional signal*. A grayscale image is an example of a two-dimensional signal. Spatial coordinates (x,y) are the two independent variables in an image. *Multidimensional signal* is a function of more than two variables. A motion picture (i.e., video) is the best example of a multidimensional signal.

Gathering Real-Time Data

Gathering the data can be conducted in two ways: manual and automated. In the manual method, the data can be collected from existing files and documents. Then, the collected data can be organized into a structured manner (i.e., a tabular format) manually. In automation, the data can be collected using some devices called *sensors*. The real-time information about the physical quantities such as temperature, pressure, images, etc., can be collected using sensors. This chapter focuses on describing automated data collection using sensors. To automate the data collection, data acquisition systems are required. This section explains how to gather data using sensors such as ultrasonic sensor, humidity, temperature, and image data from a camera. Also, storing the collected data in the structured format is discussed.

Data Acquisition

The process of sampling signals that measure real-world physical conditions and converting the resulting samples into digital numeric values that can be manipulated by a computer is called *data acquisition*. Data acquisition systems (DAS or DAQ) generally convert analog signals into digital values for processing. The data acquisition systems comprises the following three components:

- Sensors

- Signal conditioning circuitry

- Analog-to-digital converters

Sensors

Generally, sensors produce an electrical signal corresponding to the changes in the environment. A sensor is a device that converts physical parameters such as temperature, humidity, distance, etc., into an electrical signal. A sensor can be a device, module, machine, or subsystem that can detect events or changes in the environment and send the information to other electronic devices, most often a computer processor. For example, a thermocouple is a temperature sensor that produces an output voltage based on the input temperature changes. There are two types of sensors based on its output signal types: analog and digital.

Analog Sensors

Analog sensors produce a continuous output signal or voltage that is generally proportional to the quantity being measured. These sensors generally produce output signals that change smoothly and continuously over time. See Figure 4-1.

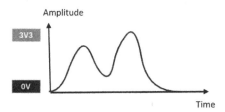

Figure 4-1. *Analog signal*

The following code continuously prints the analog value of the sensor connected to the first channel (0) of MCP3008 every second. Since MCP3008 is a 10-bit ADC, the output value ranges from 0 to 1023.

```
from gpiozero import MCP3008
from time import sleep

sensor = MCP3008(0)

while True:
    print(sensor.value)
```

Digital Sensors

Digital sensors produce digital output signals or voltages that are a digital representation of the quantity being measured. In these sensors, data conversion and data transmission take place digitally. See Figure 4-2.

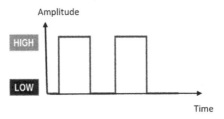

Figure 4-2. *Digital signals*

The following code prints the digital state of the GPIO pin 17 continuously:

```
from gpiozero import InputDevice
from time import sleep

sensor = InputDevice(17, pull_up=True)

while True:
    print(sensor.value)]
```

Some of the common sensors in the electronics industry are listed here:

- Temperature sensors

- IR sensors

- Ultrasonic sensors

- Pressure sensors

- Proximity sensors

- Touch sensors

- Level sensors

- Smoke and gas sensors

What Is Real-Time Data?

Real-time data (RTD) is the information that is passed along to the end user immediately after collection. The real-time data can be either static or dynamic and is generally processed using *real-time computing*.

Real-Time Data Analytics

Real-time analytics is the analysis of collected data as soon as that data is gathered. Real-time data analytics allow us to make decisions without delay and can prevent problems and issues before they occur.

Here, we are going to discuss getting real-time data about distance, humidity, temperature, and image data from a camera.

Getting Real-Time Distance Data from an Ultrasonic Sensor

The basic principle of ultrasonic sensors is to transmit and receive the sound waves. The physical variables (like distance, level, height, flow, etc.) to be measured can be calculated based on the time duration between transmitting waves and receiving echo sound waves.

Interfacing an Ultrasonic Sensor with the Raspberry Pi

Interfacing the ultrasonic sensors with Raspberry Pi was already discussed in Chapter 3. We will collect data from the HC-SR04 ultrasonic sensor, which can be used to measure the distance from 2cm to 400cm with 3mm accuracy. Here our objective is to interface an ultrasonic distance sensor with the Raspberry Pi and save the gathered data in CSV format. For that, an ultrasonic distance sensor can be connected to the Raspberry Pi GPIO pins, as shown in Figure 4-3.

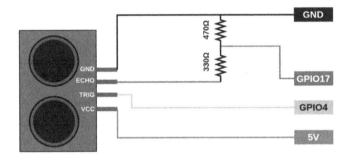

Figure 4-3. *Ultrasonic sensor connection with Raspberry Pi GPIO pins*

As covered in Chapter 3, we will use the DistanceSensor object from gpiozero library. The distance function returns the distance measured by the ultrasonic distance sensor in meters. To display in centimeters, we need to multiply the value by 100. The following code prints the distance measured by the ultrasonic distance sensor in centimeters every second and saves the collected data after 100 seconds.

```
from gpiozero import DistanceSensor
from time import sleep

sensor = DistanceSensor(echo=17, trigger=4)
```

```
n = 100
for i in range(n):
    print(sensor.distance * 100)
    sleep(1)
```

When the code is running, move the position of objects placed in front of the ultrasonic sensor to get different values. The measured distance (in cm) is printed continuously for *n* seconds; in our case, it's 100.

Getting Real-Time Image Data from a Camera

This section explains how to get real-time video from a webcam.

Getting Real-Time Video from a Webcam

Connect the USB web camera to the Raspberry Pi via the USB port. Using the OpenCV Python library, we can access the webcam and capture images and videos from it. The following code can be used to get real-time video from the webcam. The collected frames can be analyzed in real time.

```
import cv2
vid = cv2.VideoCapture(0)

while(True):

    ret, frame = vid.read()
    cv2.imshow('frame', frame)

    if cv2.waitKey(1) & 0xFF == ord('q'):
        break

vid.release()
cv2.destroyAllWindows()
```

Getting Real-Time Video from Pi-cam

Interface a Raspberry Pi camera module to the Raspberry Pi via the Camera Serial Interface (CSI) port. To enable the Raspberry Pi camera, open the Raspberry Pi configuration from the main menu and enable Camera on the Interfaces tab. The following code can be used to capture an image using the Raspberry Pi camera module and store the captured image in the specified location: /home/pi/Desktop/cammodule_img.jpg.

```
from picamera import PiCamera
from time import sleep

camera = PiCamera()

camera.start_preview()
sleep(5)
camera.capture('/home/pi/Desktop/cammodule_img.jpg')
camera.stop_preview()
```

Data Transfer

Data transmission or data transfer refers to the process of transferring data between two or more digital devices. The data is transmitted in analog or digital format, and the data transmission process enables devices or components within devices to communicate to each other.

Serial and Parallel Communication

Serial communication is the process of sending data one bit at a time, sequentially, over a communication channel or computer bus. Parallel communication is a method of conveying multiple binary digits (bits) simultaneously.

Interfacing an Arduino with the Raspberry Pi

We can connect an Arduino to a Raspberry Pi and transfer data from the Arduino to the Raspberry Pi and vice versa. The sensors, motors, and actuators can be connected to the Arduino and make the Arduino transfer values to and from the Raspberry Pi. By doing this, we can use Arduino as a node and acquire sensor data via these nodes.

Arduino can be connected to the Raspberry Pi in two ways.

- Serial communication via USB

- Serial communication via GPIO pins

Serial via USB

Using an Arduino USB cable to connect the two boards is the easiest way to establish communication between the Arduino and Raspberry Pi boards.

On the Raspberry Pi, choose any of the four USB ports available on the board and connect the USB connector. Connect the other end of the Arduino USB cable to the Arduino. The connector cable will be different for different versions of Arduino.

Serial via GPIOs

A serial connection can also be established using plain wires to connect between the Raspberry Pi GPIOs and the Arduino pins. A voltage level-shifter might be needed depending on the Arduino board you have.

The Raspberry Pi operates at 3.3V, whereas the Arduino boards such as Uno, Mega, Leonardo, Nano, etc., operate at 5V. So, a 3.3V/5V level-shifter needs to be used to protect the Raspberry Pi when connecting the RX and TX pins, as shown in Figure 4-4.

Figure 4-4. *Connection between Arduino and Raspberry Pi via GPIO pins*

Generally, the use of an Arduino USB cable is recommended over GPIOs for serial communication.

Data Transmission Between an Arduino and the Raspberry Pi

When connecting the Arduino to the Raspberry Pi via a USB cable, run the command ls /dev/tty* in the Raspberry Pi terminal window to find the name of the Arduino device. It should return something like /dev/ttyACM0 or /dev/ttyUSB0.

The pySerial Python library is used to make a serial interface with Python and encapsulates the access for the serial port.

The following code can be used to make bidirectional communication between the Arduino and the Raspberry Pi.

Arduino Code

Here is the Arduino code:

```
void setup() {
Serial.begin(9600);
}
void loop() {
  if (Serial.available() > 0) {
    String data = Serial.readStringUntil('\n');
    Serial.print("Received Data: ");
    Serial.println(data);
  }
}
```

Serial.available() will give you the number of bytes that have already arrived and are stored in the receive buffer. This can be used to check if the Arduino has received data.

If some data has arrived, Serial.readStringUntil() is used with the newline character \n to get the next line. All the bytes received until the newline character \n are automatically converted and added in an Arduino String object.

Then, we just return the string containing the received data with some additional text.

Raspberry Pi Python Code

Here is the Raspberry Pi Python code to display the serial data:

```
#!/usr/bin/env python3
import serial
import time
if __name__ == '__main__':
    ser = serial.Serial('/dev/ttyACM0', 9600, timeout=1)
```

```
ser.flush()
while True:
    ser.write(b"Data from Raspberry Pi!\n")
    line = ser.readline().decode('utf-8').rstrip()
    print(line)
    time.sleep(1)
```

The pySerial function write() is used to send data to the Arduino. Before sending the string, It will encode from string to bytes, as you can only send bytes through Serial. Any data that is not a byte or byte array must be converted before being sent through Serial.

Also, we add a newline character \n as the Arduino expects it at the end of the string while it's reading with Serial.readStringUntil('\n').

Then we read a line from Serial, decode it into a string, and finally print the received string and wait for one second before sending the next string over Serial.

Time-Series Data

A *time series* is a series of data points indexed in time order. Most commonly, it is a sequence taken at successive equally spaced points in time. Thus, a time series can be defined as a sequence of discrete-time data. In time-series data, time is often the independent variable, and the goal is generally to make a forecast for the future.

Time series are frequently plotted via line charts. Time series are used in statistics, signal processing, communications engineering, pattern recognition, weather forecasting, earthquake prediction, control engineering, astronomy, etc.

Time-Series Analysis and Forecasting

Time-series analysis comprises methods for analyzing time-series data to extract meaningful statistics and other characteristics of the data. The time-series analysis also includes forecasting the series for the future, extracting hidden signals in noisy data, discovering the data generation mechanism, etc. *Time-series forecasting* is the use of a model to predict future values based on historical data.

Memory Requirements

This section talks about the memory requirements.

More Storage

Sometimes the memory from the microSD card might not be sufficient, and more memory might be needed. More storage space can be highly beneficial to store the collected data and heavy models. To increase the storage capacity, external hard disk drives can be connected to the Raspberry Pi.

More RAM

RAM is another important factor for data science projects. The larger the RAM, the higher the amount of data it can handle, which results in faster processing. Although the base variant of 1GB RAM can do the job, the 4GB RAM version of the Raspberry Pi is recommended for most deep learning tasks.

Case Study: Gathering the Real-Time Industry Data

Let's look at a case study.

Storing Collected Data Using Pandas

The collected data can also be saved for later use. Pandas is an open source data analysis and manipulation tool built in Python. We will use Pandas to convert the collected data into a structured data format. The Pandas library can be installed via `pip` using the following command:

```
pip install pandas
```

Dataframes

A *dataframe* is a two-dimensional data structure. Data is aligned in a tabular fashion in rows and columns, and it is generally the most commonly used Pandas object. Once we convert our data into dataframes, we can easily manipulate and export the data to other formats such as CSV and Microsoft Excel.

Saving Data as a CSV File

A comma-separated values file is a delimited text file that uses a comma to separate values. Each line of the file is a data record. Each record consists of one or more fields, separated by commas. A Pandas dataframe's `to_csv()` function exports the dataframe to CSV format.

```
df.to_csv('file path\File Name.csv')
```

Saving as an Excel File

To write a single object to an Excel .xlsx file, it is only necessary to specify a target filename. To write multiple sheets, it is necessary to create an ExcelWriter object with a target filename and specify a sheet in the file to write to. The Pandas dataframe's to_excel() function exports the dataframe to .xlsx format.

```
df.to_excel("output.xlsx")
```

Reading Saved Data Files

Once the data is saved, it can be read using the read_csv() or read_excel() function. The read_excel() function reads an Excel file into a Pandas dataframe, and it supports the .xls, .xlsx, .xlsm, .xlsb, and .odf file extensions read from a local filesystem or URL. It has an option to read a single sheet or a list of sheets. The read_csv() function reads a CSV file into a dataframe and also supports optionally iterating or breaking of the file into chunks.

Adding the Date and Time to the Real-Time Data

While collecting the data, we can also add the data and time to the data. We will use the datetime Python library. datetime.datetime.now() can be used to get the current date and time.

```
from datetime import datetime
now = datetime.now()

print("now =", now)

# dd/mm/YY H:M:S
dt_string = now.strftime("%d/%m/%Y %H:%M:%S")
print("date and time =", dt_string)
```

Industry Data from the Temperature and Humidity Sensor

We will use the temperature and humidity sensor to measure the temperature and humidity. Connect the DHT 11/22 sensor module to the Raspberry Pi as shown in Chapter 3.

The following code collects the temperature and humidity values for 100 seconds and stores the collected data as a CSV file:

```
import Adafruit_DHT
import time
from datetime import datetime

DHT_SENSOR = Adafruit_DHT.DHT11
DHT_PIN = 17

data = []

while _ in range(100):

    humidity, temperature = Adafruit_DHT.read(DHT_SENSOR,
    DHT_PIN)

    if humidity is not None and temperature is not None:

      now = datetime.now()
      dt_string = now.strftime("%d/%m/%Y %H:%M:%S")

      data.append(dt_string,humidity,temperature)

    time.sleep(60*5)

df = pd.DataFrame(data)
df.to_csv('data.csv',index=None,header=None)
```

The CSV file will look as follows:

17/05/2020 01:05:14	26.24	69.91
17/05/2020 01:10:14	26.24	70.65
17/05/2020 01:15:14	26.22	68.87
17/05/2020 01:20:14	26.15	70.11
17/05/2020 01:25:14	26.11	69.02

CHAPTER 5

Preparing the Data

The most important step in data science is to prepare the data. Data preparation is the process of cleaning, processing, and transforming the raw data for analysis. From this stage, the errors in the data can be effectively handled by cleaning, identifying the missing values, handling outliers, etc. Hence, this chapter discusses the methodologies used to prepare the data using the Pandas package in Python.

Pandas and Data Structures

Pandas is a software library written for the Python programming language that is used mainly for data manipulation and analysis.

In a nutshell, Pandas is like Excel for Python, with tables (which in Pandas are called *dataframes*) made of rows and columns (which in Pandas are called *series*). Pandas has many functionalities that make it an awesome library for data processing, inspection, and manipulation.

Installing and Using Pandas

Installing Pandas on your system requires NumPy to be installed, and if building the library from source, it requires the appropriate tools to compile the C and Cython sources on which Pandas is built.

© K. Mohaideen Abdul Kadhar and G. Anand 2021
K. M. Abdul Kadhar and G. Anand, *Data Science with Raspberry Pi*,
https://doi.org/10.1007/978-1-4842-6825-4_5

You can find details about this installation in the Pandas documentation. Pandas can be installed using pip function as: pip install pandas. Once Pandas is installed, you can import it and check the version, as shown here:

```
import pandas
pandas.__version__
```

Just as we generally import NumPy under the alias np, we will import Pandas under the alias pd, and this import convention will be used throughout the remainder of this book.

```
import pandas as pd
```

Pandas Data Structures

A data structure is a data organization, management, and storage format that enables efficient access and modification. More precisely, a data structure is a collection of data values, the relationships among them, and the functions or operations that can be applied to the data. Pandas introduces two new data structures to Python, Series and DataFrame, both of which are built on top of NumPy (which means they are fast).

Series

A *series* is a one-dimensional object similar to an array, list, or column in a table. It will assign a labeled index to each item in the series. By default, each item will receive an index label from 0 to N, where N is the length of the series minus 1, as illustrated here:

```
s = pd.Series([1, 'Raspberry Pi', 3.14, -500, 'Data'])
print(s)
```

Output:

```
0           1
1    Raspberry Pi
2    3.14
3    -500
4    Data
dtype: object
```

Instead of providing the default index, we can specify an index to be used for each entry while creating the series, as illustrated here:

```
s = pd.Series([1, 'Raspberry Pi', 3.14, -500, 'Data'],
               index=['M', 'A', 'X', 'I', 'E'])
print(s)
Output:
M           1
A    Raspberry Pi
X    3.14
I    -500
E    Data
dtype: object
```

The Series constructor can convert a dictionary into a series as well, using the keys of the dictionary as its index, as illustrated here:

```
d = {'English': 95, 'Math': 100, 'Science': 98, 'Social
Science': 93}
marks = pd.Series(d)
print(marks)
Output:
English           95
Math              100
```

```
Science            98
Social Science     93
dtype: float64
```

The index can be used to select specific items from the series. For instance, the marks for math can be selected by specifying the index Math. Similarly, a group of items can be printed by providing their corresponding indices separated by commas in a list, as illustrated here:

```
print (marks['Math'])
print(marks[['English', 'Science', 'Social Science']])

Output :
100.0
English            95
Science            98
Social Science     93
dtype: float64
```

Boolean indexing for filtering values can also be used. For example, using the index marks < 96 returns a series of Boolean values, which we then pass to our series marks, returning the corresponding True items, as illustrated here:

```
marks[marks < 96]
Output:
Math               100
Science            98
dtype: float64
```

The value of a particular item in the series can be changed on the go by accessing the corresponding index of the item, as illustrated here:

```
print('Old value:', marks['Math'])
marks['Math'] = 99
```

```
print('New value:', marks['Math'])
Output:
('Old value:', 100.0)
('New value:', 99.0)
```

We can also check whether an item exists in the series or not using the following code:

```
print('Math' in marks)
print('French' in marks)
Output:
True
False
```

Mathematical operations can also be done on a series of numerical values, as illustrated here:

```
marks * 10
Output:
English          950
Math             990
Science          980
Social Science   930
dtype: float64
```

```
np.square(marks)
Output:
English          9025
Math             9801
Science          9604
Social Science   8649
dtype: float64
```

DataFrame

The tabular DataFrame data structure is composed of rows and columns, similar to a spreadsheet or a database table. You can also think of a DataFrame as a group of Series objects that share an index (the column names).

Reading Data

To create a DataFrame data structure out of common Python data structures, we can pass a dictionary of lists to the DataFrame constructor.

```
a={'Name':['Augustus', 'Hazel', 'Esther', 'Cavas'],
     'Gender':['Male','Female','Female','Male'],
     'Age':[19, 18, 22, 21]}
b=pd.DataFrame.from_dict(a)
          print(b)
```

```
Output:
   Name       Gender   Age
0  Augustus     Male   19
1     Hazel   Female   18
2    Esther   Female   22
3     Cavas     Male   21
```

Reading CSV Data

Reading a CSV file is as simple as calling the read_csv function. By default, the read_csv function expects the column separator to be a comma, but you can change that using the sep parameter. The following code shows the syntax to read a CSV file into a DataFrame 'df' and print the first five rows of df using the head() function:

```
df = pd.read_csv('data.csv')
print(df.head())
```

There's also a set of writer functions for writing the DataFrame object to a variety of formats such as CSV files, HTML tables, JSON, etc. The following line of code shows the syntax to write a DataFrame object to a CSV file:

```
df.to_csv('path_to_file.csv')
```

Reading Excel Data

Pandas allows us to read and write Excel files, so we can easily read from Excel, in Python, and then write the data back out to Excel. Reading Excel files requires the xlrd library, which can be installed using the pip command, as shown here:

pip install xlrd.

The following code illustrates the syntax used to read a sheet from an Excel file into a DataFrame df. Replace data.xlsx with the path/filename of your Excel file to run the code.

```
df = pd.read_excel('data.xlsx', 'Sheet1')
print(df.head())
```

Similarly, the data from a `DataFrame` object can be written to an Excel file, as shown here:

```
dataframe.to_excel('path_to_file.xlsx', index=False)
```

Reading URL Data

The `read_table` function can be used to read directly from a URL. The following code illustrates a `DataFrame` created using raw data from a given URL:

```
url = 'https://raw.github.com/gjreda/best-sandwiches/master/
data/best-sandwiches-geocode.tsv'
from_url = pd.read_table(url, sep='\t')
from_url.head(3)
Output:
      rank              sandwich  ...  lat        lng
0     1                     BLT  ...  41.895734  -87.679960
1     2          Fried Bologna  ...  41.884672  -87.647754
2     3      Woodland Mushroom  ...  41.890602  -87.630925
```

Cleaning the Data

In most of the data analytics projects, the available data is not always perfect. The raw data always tends to be messy with corrupt or inaccurate data in addition to the useful data. It is therefore essential for the data scientists to treat these messy data samples so as to convert the raw data to a form which can work, and they spend a considerably long time doing so.

Data cleaning is the process of identifying inaccurate, incorrect, or incomplete parts of the data and treating them by replacing, deleting, or modifying the data. In other words, it is the process of preparing the data for analysis by treating all the irregularities in the raw data. In the following sections, we will discuss how to handle missing values and outliers, fill in the inappropriate values, and remove duplicate entries.

Handling Missing Values

Missing values are quite common in raw data. Assume that the input data consists of product feedback from thousands of customers collected using survey forms. It is common behavior for customers to skip a few entries while filling out the survey forms. For instance, a few customers may not share their experience with the product, some may not share the duration for which they have been using the product, and a few others may not fill their contact information. While compiling these survey forms and converting them into a table, there is sure to be plenty of missing values in the table.

Data from sensors may also have missing data due to various reasons like a temporary power outage at the sensor node, hardware failure, interference in communication, etc. Therefore, handling these missing values is the foremost task for data scientists while dealing with raw data. The following code illustrates the creation of a database of random numbers using the random.randn function in the NumPy library:

```
import pandas as pd
import numpy as np
df = pd.DataFrame(np.random.randn(6,4),
index = ['1','3','4','6','7','9'], columns = ['a','b','c','d'])
```

It can be seen from the previous code that the indices for rows and columns have been allocated manually. From the indices allotted for rows, it can be seen that indexes 2, 5, and 8 are missing. Using the reindex function in the Pandas library, these indices are created with missing 'Not a Number' (NaN) values, as illustrated here:

```
df=df.reindex(['1','2','3','4','5','6','7','8','9'])
print(df)
Output:
          a          b          c          d
1   0.099344   0.293956   1.002970   0.516942
2        NaN        NaN        NaN        NaN
3   1.608906  -1.748396  -1.013634  -0.651055
4   3.211263  -2.555312  -1.036068  -0.728020
5        NaN        NaN        NaN        NaN
6  -0.101766  -0.205572   1.369707  -1.133026
7   0.062344   1.483505   0.026995   1.560656
8        NaN        NaN        NaN        NaN
9  -0.324347  -0.342040   0.107224   0.272153
```

Now that a database with missing values has been created, the next step is to treat these values. Before considering the options for treating these values, the foremost task is to detect the location of the missing values. The isnull() function in the Pandas library can be used to detect the rows containing missing values, as illustrated here:

```
df1=df[df.isna().any(axis=1)]
print(df1)
Output:
     a    b    c    d
2  NaN  NaN  NaN  NaN
5  NaN  NaN  NaN  NaN
8  NaN  NaN  NaN  NaN
```

The previous process gives us a fair idea of the amount of missing data in our database. Once this missing data is detected, the next step is to treat the missing data. There are two ways we can do this: one is to fill the missing data with values, and the second one is to simply remove the missing data.

The `fillna()` function in the Pandas library can be used to fill the missing values with a user-specified scalar value, as illustrated here. As shown, the missing values in rows 2 and 5 are replaced by 0.000000.

```
df2=df.fillna(0)
print(df2.head())
Output:
         a         b         c         d
1  0.099344  0.293956  1.002970  0.516942
2  0.000000  0.000000  0.000000  0.000000
3  1.608906 -1.748396 -1.013634 -0.651055
4  3.211263 -2.555312 -1.036068 -0.728020
5  0.000000  0.000000  0.000000  0.000000
```

Another way to replace the missing values is to use the `ffill` or `bfill` function in the Pandas library. `ffill` stands for "forward fill," which fills the missing values by repeating the values that occur before them, and `bfill` stands for "backward fill," which fills the missing values by repeating the values that occur after them. The following code illustrates the forward fill approach of filling in the missing values:

```
df3= df.fillna(method='ffill')
print(df3.head())
Output:
         a         b         c         d
1  0.099344  0.293956  1.002970  0.516942
2  0.099344  0.293956  1.002970  0.516942
```

```
3   1.608906 -1.748396 -1.013634 -0.651055
4   3.211263 -2.555312 -1.036068 -0.728020
5   3.211263 -2.555312 -1.036068 -0.728020
```

The second possible way to deal with missing values is to simply drop them by using the dropna function in the Pandas library, as illustrated here:

```
df4=df.dropna()
print(df4)
Output:
          a         b         c         d
1   0.099344  0.293956  1.002970  0.516942
3   1.608906 -1.748396 -1.013634 -0.651055
4   3.211263 -2.555312 -1.036068 -0.728020
6  -0.101766 -0.205572  1.369707 -1.133026
7   0.062344  1.483505  0.026995  1.560656
9  -0.324347 -0.342040  0.107224  0.272153
```

We have created a simple dataset with missing values to understand the concept of treating the missing values. In reality, the datasets used in analytics projects are large and may easily contain 500 to 1,000 rows or even more. You are encouraged to apply the learning from this example on real datasets. The method for treating missing values may depend on the nature of application as well as on the number or frequency of missing values in the dataset.

Handling Outliers

In a dataset, outliers are the observations (i.e data) that stand out from all the other observations. In other words, *outliers* are data points that are distant from all the other data in the dataset. Outliers can originate either due to errors in measurement/data entry or due to genuine extreme values in the data. For instance, consider the series of numbers 112, 123, 120, 132, 106, 26, 118, 140, and 125. In this series, all the numbers are close to 100 except 26. Hence, 26 is an outlier as it is vastly distant from the rest of the numbers.

Outliers can be detected in two ways: using visualization techniques and using a mathematical approach. In this section, we introduce two mathematical approaches to identify outliers in our data, namely, interquartile range (IQR) and the Z-score.

Interquartile range is a measure of the variability or spread of data in a dataset. The data is first ordered and divided into four quarters. The values that divide the total range into four quarters are called *quartiles*. Therefore, there will be three quartiles for splitting data into four quarters. The quartiles are Q_1, Q_2, and Q_3, where Q_2 is the median for the entire data, Q_1 is the median for the upper half of the data, and Q_3 is the median for the lower half of the data. IQR is the difference between the third quartile and first quartile, i.e., $Q_3 - Q_1$.

To illustrate the process of removing outliers using IQR, let's first create a DataFrame with 15 entries that includes outliers.

```
import pandas as pd
a={'Name':['A','B','C','D','E','F','G','H','I','J','K','L',
    'M','N','O'],
    'Weight':[56,62,48,72,15,80,76,64,68,180,75,47,58,63,71]}
df=pd.DataFrame.from_dict(a)
print(df.head())
```
Output:
```
  Name  Weight
0   A      56
1   B      62
2   C      48
3   D      72
4   E      25
```

In the previous code, we created a database containing the weight in kilograms of 15 adults. For convenience, we have named the adults with the letters *A* to *M*. Weights of 15kg and 180kg have been included as outliers as it is unlikely for healthy adults to weigh so little or much. To detect these outliers, we need to compute the 25 percent and 75 percent quartile values, Q1 and Q3, respectively. From these values, the IQR value can be calculated by determining the difference of Q3 – Q1. This process is illustrated here:

```
Q1=df.Weight.quantile(0.25)
Q3=df.Weight.quantile(0.75)
IQR=Q3-Q1
print('Q1=',Q1,'Q3=',Q3,'IQR=',IQR)
Output:
Q1= 57.0 Q3= 73.5 IQR= 16.5
```

By comparing the entries in the DataFrame object with the quartiles calculated previously, it can be seen that there are four values below Q1, seven values between Q1 and Q3, and four values above Q3. But we know that there is only one outlier below Q1 and one outlier above Q3. To detect those outliers, we need to form an interval with a lower limit much below Q1 and an upper limit well above Q3. Once these limits are established, then it will be safe to consider that the values below the lower limit and the values above the upper limit will be outliers. This is illustrated in the following code:

```
lower_limit = Q1 - 1.5 * IQR
upper_limit = Q3 + 1.5 * IQR
df1=df[(df.Weight < lower_limit) | (df.Weight > upper_limit)]
print(df1)
Output:
    Name  Weight
4    E      25
9    J     180
```

It can be seen that the limits created using the IQR value have detected the outliers in our data accurately. Now these outliers can be easily filtered out using the following code:

```
df2=df.drop(df1.index)
    print(df2)
Output:
```

	Name	Weight
0	A	56
1	B	62
2	C	48
3	D	72
5	F	80
6	G	76
7	H	64
8	I	68
10	K	75
11	L	47
12	M	58
13	N	63
14	O	71

Z-Score

The Z-score, also called the *standard score*, gives an idea of how far away a data point is from the mean value. Technically, the Z-score fits the data in a normal distribution and measures the number of standard deviations by which the data points are about the mean value of the entire dataset, as illustrated in Figure 5-1.

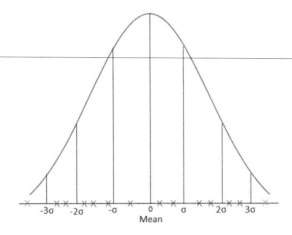

Figure 5-1. *Normal distribution of data for outlier detection based on the Z-score*

The Figure 5-1 shows that each data point is mapped along a normal distribution centered at the zero mean. The data points that are too far from the zero mean are treated as outliers. In the majority of cases, the threshold is fixed as 3, and any data point beyond 3σ or -3σ is treated as an outlier. Let's take the same database that we used in the previous section and identify the outliers using the Z-score.

```
import pandas as pd
from scipy import stats
import numpy as np
a={'Name':['A','B','C','D','E','F','G','H','I','J','K','L',
    'M','N','O'],
    'Weight':[56,62,48,72,15,80,76,64,68,180,75,47,58,63,71,]}
df=pd.DataFrame.from_dict(a)
z = np.abs(stats.zscore(df.Weight))
print(z)
df1=df[z>3]
print(df1)
```

Output:
```
    Name  Weight
9    J      180
```

From the previous code, it can be seen that the Z-score corresponding to the weight value of 180 exceeds the threshold of 3, and hence it is displayed as an outlier. Unfortunately, the weight value of 15 is not detected as an outlier. The reason for this could be understood by comparing the value with respect to the mean and standard deviation, which can be achieved through the np.mean and np.std functions, as illustrated here:

```
print(np.mean(df.Weight))
print(np.std(df.Weight))
Output:
67.0
33.448467827390836
```

Let's approximate the value of standard deviation as 33.45. It can be seen that the difference between the weight value 180 and the mean value is 111, which is greater than three times the standard deviation ($>3\sigma$), whereas the difference between the weight values 15 and the mean value is just 54, which is less than two times the standard deviation ($<2\sigma$). One way to overcome this problem is to reduce the value of threshold. Let's assume a Threshold value of 1.

```
df1=df[z>1]
    print(df1)
Output:
    Name  Weight
4    E      15
9    J      180
```

From the previous illustration, it can be seen that the ideal threshold of 3 may not hold true for every dataset, and hence the threshold should be selected based on the distribution of the data. Now similar to the case of IQR, these outliers can be simply filtered out using the following code:

```
df2=df.drop(df.Name[z>1].index)
print(df2)
Output:
      Name  Weight
0      A      56
1      B      62
2      C      48
3      D      72
5      F      80
6      G      76
7      H      64
8      I      68
10     K      75
11     L      47
12     M      58
13     N      63
14     O      71
```

Filtering Out Inappropriate Values

In some cases, the dataset may contain some inappropriate values that are completely irrelevant to the data. This is especially true in the case of sensor data. The data recorded from the sensor is normally time-series data with a unique timestamp for each data point. These timestamps

are not required for analysis in many cases and hence can be treated as
inappropriate values. To illustrate this concept, we create a time-series
temperature data similar to the sensor data as follows:

```
import pandas as pd
data={'Time':['12:00:05','12:08:33','12:25:12','12:37:53',
'12:59:08'],
      'Temperature':['T=22','T=22','T=23','T=23','T=24']}
df=pd.DataFrame.from_dict(data)
print(df)
Output:
        Time Temperature
0   12:00:05        T=22
1   12:08:33        T=22
2   12:25:12        T=23
3   12:37:53        T=23
4   12:59:08        T=24
```

Now, the timestamp corresponding to each data point and the header
'T=' in each data point should be removed. The timestamp can be removed
using the drop function in the Pandas library, whereas the header can be
removed by using the str.replace function. Because of the presence of a
header in each data point, the data is initially stored as a string data type.
So, the datatype has to be changed to int or float after removing these
headers. These procedures are illustrated as follows:

```
df.drop('Time',inplace=True,axis=1)
df=df.Temperature.str.replace('T=','')
df=df.astype(float)
print(df)
Output:
0       22.0
1       22.0
```

```
2    23.0
3    23.0
4    24.0
Name: Temperature, dtype: float64
```

Removing Duplicates

Duplicate entries are common in data science, especially when we collect data from various sources and consolidate them for processing. Depending on the nature of our analysis, these duplicates may pose a problem. Therefore, it is better to remove these duplicates before analyzing the data, as illustrated here:

```
import pandas as pd
a={'Name':['Alan','Joe','Jim','Tom','Alan','Anna','Elle','Rachel','
Mindy'],
    'Age':[22,24,25,24,22,23,21,22,23]}
df=pd.DataFrame.from_dict(a)
print('DATA\n',df)
print('DUPLICATES\n',df[df.duplicated()])
df1=df.drop_duplicates()
print('DATA AFTER REMOVING DUPLICATES\n',df1)
```

```
Output:
DATA
      Name  Age
0     Alan   22
1      Joe   24
2      Jim   25
3      Tom   24
4     Alan   22
5     Anna   23
```

```
6    Ellen    21
7    Rachel   22
8    Mindy    23
DUPLICATES
     Name    Age
4    Alan    22
DATA AFTER REMOVING DUPLICATES
     Name    Age
0    Alan    22
1    Joe     24
2    Jim     25
3    Tom     24
5    Anna    23
6    Ellen   21
7    Rachel  22
8    Mindy   23
```

As shown in the code, a DataFrame is created from a dictionary consisting of the name and age of a few people, and we have deliberately created a duplicate entry for the name Alan. It can be seen that the *duplicated* function in the Pandas library clearly identifies the second entry for this name. This duplicate entry is then removed by using the drop_duplicates function in the Pandas library.

CHAPTER 6

Visualizing the Data

In the previous chapter, we discussed a number of steps involved in preparing the data for analysis. Before analyzing the data, it is imperative to get to know the nature of data we are dealing with. Visualizing the data may give us some useful insights about the nature of data. These insights, such as patterns in the data, distribution of the data, outliers present in the data, etc., can prove to be handy in determining the methodology to be used for analyzing the data. In addition, visualization can be used at the end of analysis to communicate the findings to the party concerned, as conveying the results of analysis through visualization techniques can be more effective than writing pages of textual content explaining the findings. In this chapter, we will learn about some of the basic visualization plots provided by the Matplotlib package of Python and how those plots can be customized to convey the characteristics of different data.

Matplotlib Library

Matplotlib is a plotting library for creating publication-quality plots using the Python programming language. This package provides various types of plots based on the type of information to be conveyed. The plots come with interactive options such as pan, zoom, and subplot configurations. The plots can also be saved in different formats such as PNG, PDF, etc. In addition, the Matplotlib package provides numerous customization options for each type of plot that can be used for effective representation of the information to be conveyed.

© K. Mohaideen Abdul Kadhar and G. Anand 2021
K. M. Abdul Kadhar and G. Anand, *Data Science with Raspberry Pi*,
https://doi.org/10.1007/978-1-4842-6825-4_6

Scatter Plot

A scatter plot is a type of plot that uses markers to indicate data points to show the relationship between two variables. The scatter plot can serve many purposes when it comes to data analysis. For example, the plot can reveal patterns and trends in data when the data points are taken as whole, which in turn can help data scientists understand the relationship between two variables and hence enable them to come up with an effective prediction technique. Scatter plots can also be used for identifying clusters in the data. They can also reveal outliers present in the data, which is crucial as outliers tend to drastically affect the performance of prediction systems.

Two columns of data are generally required to create scatter plots, one for each dimension of the plot. Each row of data in the table will correspond to a single data point in the plot. A scatter plot can be created using the scatter function in the Matplotlib library. To demonstrate the usefulness of scatter plots, let's consider the Boston Housing dataset that can be imported from the Scikit-Learn library. This dataset is actually taken from the StatLib library, which is maintained at Carnegie Mellon University. It consists of 506 samples with 13 different feature attributes such as per capita crime rate by town (CRIM), average number of rooms per dwelling (RM), index of accessibility to radial highways (RAD), etc. In addition, a target attribute MEDV indicates the median value of owner-occupied homes in the thousands.

The following code illustrates the process of creating a Pandas dataframe the Boston housing dataset, which is originally in a dictionary format. For convenience, only the first five rows of the dataframe are displayed in this code using the print command.

```
import matplotlib.pyplot as plt
import numpy as np
import pandas as pd
from sklearn.datasets import load_boston
dataset = load_boston()
boston_data=pd.DataFrame(dataset.data,columns=dataset.feature_
names)
print(boston_data.head())
```

Output:

```
   CRIM   ZN   INDUS  CHAS  NOX  ...  RAD  TAX  PTRATIO    B   LSTAT
0  0.00632  18.0  2.31  0.0  0.538  ...  1.0  296.0  15.3  396.90  4.98
1  0.02731   0.0  7.07  0.0  0.469  ...  2.0  242.0  17.8  396.90  9.14
2  0.02729   0.0  7.07  0.0  0.469  ...  2.0  242.0  17.8  392.83  4.03
3  0.03237   0.0  2.18  0.0  0.458  ...  3.0  222.0  18.7  394.63  2.94
4  0.06905   0.0  2.18  0.0  0.458  ...  3.0  222.0  18.7  396.90  5.33
[5 rows x 13 columns]
```

The housing dataset is originally in the form of a dictionary, and it is saved to the variable dataset. The 13 feature attributes are assigned to the key data, and the target attribute MEDV is assigned to the key target. The 13 features are then converted to a Pandas dataframe. Now, the scatter plot of the feature variable RM versus the target variable MEDV can be obtained by the following code. From the plot in Figure 6-1, we can see that the price of a house increases with the increase in the number of rooms. In addition to this trend, a few outliers can also be seen in the plot.

```
plt.scatter(boston_data['RM'],dataset.target)
plt.xlabel("Average number of rooms per dwelling(RM)")
plt.ylabel("Median value of owner-occupied homes in
$1000s(MEDV)")
plt.show()
```

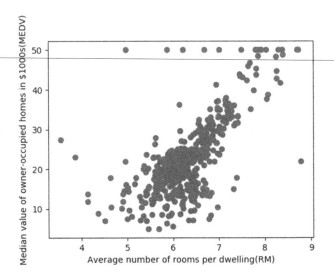

Figure 6-1. *Plot of pricing of houses versus average number of rooms per dwelling*

Line Plot

A line plot is nothing but a series of data points connected by a line, and it can be used to convey the trend of a variable over a particular time. Line plots are often used for visualizing time-series data to observe the variation of data with respect to time. It can also be used as part of the analysis procedure to check the variation of a variable in an iterative process.

Line plots can be obtained using the plot function in the Matplotlib package. To demonstrate a line plot, let's consider a time-series dataset consisting of the minimum daily temperature in ^{0}C over 10 years (1981–1990) in the city of Melbourne, Australia. The following code illustrates the process of loading the .csv file containing the dataset, converting it into a dataframe, and plotting the variation in temperature for 1981.

```
import pandas as pd
import matplotlib.pyplot as plt
import numpy as np
dataset=pd.read_csv('daily-min-temperatures.csv')
df=pd.DataFrame(dataset,columns=['Date','Temp'])
print(df.head())
```

Output:

```
            Date    Temp
0       1981-01-01    20.7
1       1981-01-02    17.9
2       1981-01-03    18.8
3       1981-01-04    14.6
4       1981-01-05    15.8
```

```
plt.plot(df['Temp'][0:365])
plt.xlabel("Days in the year")
plt.ylabel("Temperature in degree celcius")
plt.show()
```

The line plot in Figure 6-2 clearly shows the day-to-day variation of temperature in Melbourne in 1981.

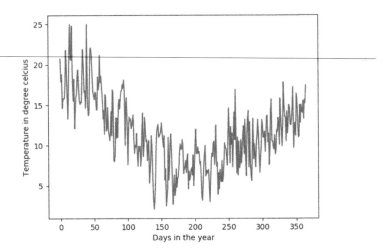

Figure 6-2. *Variation in temperature (⁰C) in Melbourne over the year 1981*

The Matplotlib package also provides the option of subplots wherein a layout of subplots can be created in a single-figure object. In this time-series data example, we can use a simple for loop to extract the data for each of the 10 years and plot it in individual subplots, as illustrated by the following code:

```
y,k=0,1
x=np.arange(1,366)
for i in range(10):
        plt.subplot(10,1,k)
        plt.plot(x,df['Temp'][y:y+365])
        y=y+365
        k=k+1
plt.xlabel("Days in the year")
plt.show()
```

Figure 6-3 consists of 10 subplots each displaying the variation of temperature over a particular year from 1981 to 1990. Thus, the use of multiple subplots has enabled us to compare the trends in temperature variation in Melbourne over the decade.

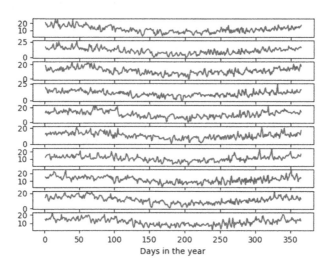

Figure 6-3. *Temperature variation in Melbourne over 10 years (1981 to 1990)*

Histogram

Histogram plots work by splitting the data in a variable into different ranges, called *bins*; then they count the data points in each bin and plot them as vertical bars. These types of plots can give a good idea about the approximate distribution of numerical data. The width of the bins, i.e., the range of values in each bin, is an important parameter, and the one that best fits the data has to be selected by trying out different values.

To demonstrate the histogram plot, let's consider the California housing dataset that is available in the Scikit-Learn library. This dataset, derived from the 1990 U.S. Census, uses one row per census block group. A block group is the smallest geographical unit for which the U.S. Census

Bureau publishes sample data (a block group typically has a population of 600 to 3,000 people). The dataset consists of 8 parameters such as median income in block, median house age in block, average number of rooms, etc., and one target attribute, which is the median house value for California districts. There are a total of 20,640 data points (rows) in the data. The following code plots a histogram that shows the distribution of blocks based on the median age of houses within the blocks. Figure 6-4 shows the histogram plot. A lower number normally suggests a newer building.

```
import matplotlib.pyplot as plt
from sklearn.datasets import fetch_california_housing
import pandas as pd
dataset = fetch_california_housing()
df=pd.DataFrame(dataset.data,columns=dataset.feature_names)
print(df.head())
```

```
Output:
     MedInc  HouseAge   AveRooms   ...  AveOccup  Latitude  Longitude
0    8.3252     41.0    6.984127   ...  2.555556     37.88    -122.23
1    8.3014     21.0    6.238137   ...  2.109842     37.86    -122.22
2    7.2574     52.0    8.288136   ...  2.802260     37.85    -122.24
3    5.6431     52.0    5.817352   ...  2.547945     37.85    -122.25
4    3.8462     52.0    6.281853   ...  2.181467     37.85    -122.25
plt.hist(df['HouseAge'],bins=20)
plt.xlabel("median age of houses")
plt.ylabel("Frequency")
plt.show()
```

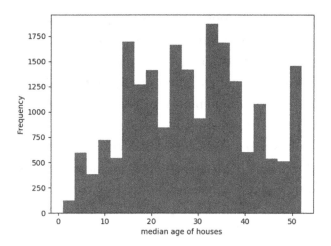

Figure 6-4. *Distribution of blocks based on median age of houses in the blocks*

From the histogram plot in Figure 6-4, we can see that most houses in the blocks are distributed in the middle, which indicates that the number of new blocks and very old blocks are lower compared to those with an average age.

Bar Chart

Bar charts are often used by data scientists in their presentations and reports to represent categorical data as horizontal or vertical rectangular bars whose length or height corresponds to the value of the data that they represent. Normally, one of the axes will represent the category of data, while the other axis will represent the corresponding values. Therefore, bar graphs are the ideal choice for comparing different categories of data. Bar charts can also be used for conveying the development of one or multiple variables over a period of time.

Even though bar charts look similar to histogram plots, there are subtle differences between them. For instance, histograms are used to plot the distribution of variables, and bar charts are used to compare variables belonging to different categories. A histogram groups quantitative data into a finite number of bins and plots the distribution of data in those bins, whereas bar charts are used to plot categorical data.

To demonstrate the bar chart, let's consider the Telecoms Consumer Complaints dataset, which is a collection of complaints received by Comcast, an American global telecommunication company. This company was fined $2.3 million in October 2016 over numerous customer complaints claiming that they have been charged for services they never used. This dataset is a collection of 2,224 such complaints categorized into 11 columns such as customer complaint, date, city, state, ZIP code, status, etc. In the following code, the dataset available as an Excel sheet is first loaded and converted to a dataframe. Then the column containing the states, from which the complaints are received, is selected, and the multiple entries corresponding to the same states are grouped together to a single entry using the function groupby(). The count of the number of times each state is repeated, which in turn corresponds to the number of complaints received from each state, is obtained by using the function size(). The data can then be sorted in descending order of the count values using the function sort_values(). Figure 6-5 shows the plot of top 10 states with the most number of complaints, which gives a clear idea of where more customers have faced grievances. The plot basically gives a comparison of the company's misgivings in different states based on the number of complaints received from the customers.

```
import pandas as pd
import matplotlib.pyplot as plt
dataset=pd.read_excel('Comcast_telecom_complaints_data.csv.xlsx')
data=pd.DataFrame(dataset)
print(data.head(3))
```

```
Output:
   Ticket #          Customer Complaint   ...   Zip code  Status
0  250635  Comcast Cable Internet Speeds   ...     21009  Closed
1  223441  Payment disappear - service got disconnected ... 30102  Closed
2  242732              Speed and Service   ...     30101  Closed
[3 rows x 11 columns]
```

```
a=data.groupby("State").size().sort_values(ascending=False).
reset_index()
plt.bar(a['State'][0:10],a[0][0:10],align='center')
plt.show()
```

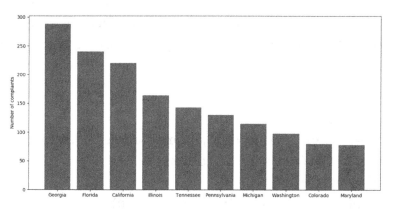

Figure 6-5. Bar plot showing number of complaints received from different states

131

Pie Chart

Pie charts are generally used to show the distribution of data across different categories as a percentage of the entire data in the form of proportional circular segments. In other words, each circular segment corresponds to a particular category of data. By viewing pie charts, users can quickly grasp the distribution of categorical data by just visualizing the plot rather than seeing the percentage in numbers as in the case of bar plots. Another difference between pie chart and bar charts is that pie charts are used to compare the contribution of each category of data to the whole, whereas bar charts are used to compare the contribution of different categories of data against each other.

To demonstrate a pie chart, let's consider a dataset containing the details of immigration to Canada from 1980 to 2013. The dataset contains various attributes for immigrants both entering and leaving Canada annually. These attributes include origin/destination name, area name, region name, etc. There are a total of 197 rows of data based on the origin/destination of the immigrants. The following code plots a pie chart that shows the total number of immigrants from 1980 to 2013 categorized by their continent:

```
import pandas as pd
import matplotlib.pyplot as plt
df = pd.read_excel('Canada.xlsx',skiprows=range(20),skipfooter=2)
df.columns = list(map(str, df.columns))
df['Total']=df.sum(axis=1)
df_continents = df.groupby('AreaName', axis=0).sum().reset_index()
print(df_continents)
```

Output:

	AreaName	AREA	REG	...	2012
2013	Total				
0	Africa	48762	49242	...	38083
38543	765660				
1	Asia	45815	109147	...	152218
155075	3516953				
2	Europe	39044	39754	...	29177
28691	1528488				
3 Latin	America and the Caribbean	29832	30395	...	27173
24950	855141				
4	Northern America	1810	1810	...	7892
8503	246564				
5	Oceania	12726	13210	...	1679
1775	93736				

After the dataset is loaded as a Pandas dataframe, the column titles with numbers indicating the year of data are converted to string format. This is done to ensure that the titles are not added when we sum across the rows to compute the total number of immigrants in the next step. This total number of immigrants is saved in an additional column created in the name Total. After computing the total number of immigrants, the data is grouped by the column titled AreaName containing the continent details of the immigrants. By doing this, the number of rows is now reduced to 6 from 197, which indicates that the entire dataset is grouped into 6 continents.

Now the total number of immigrants from the six continents, given in the column titled Total, can be plotted as a pie chart shown in Figure 6-6. Therefore, the pie chart will contain six circular segments corresponding to the six continents. To label these segments in the plot, the continent names present in the column titled AreaName is converted to a list and stored in a variable to be used as labels in the plot function. This code is illustrated here:

```
t=list(df_continents.AreaName)
plt.pie(df_continents['Total'],labels=t,autopct='%1.1f%%',
shadow=True)
plt.show()
```

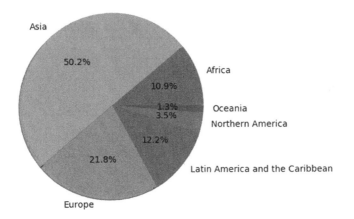

Figure 6-6. *Pie chart indicating movement of immigrants belonging to different continents into and out of Canada from 1980 to 2013*

Other Plots and Packages

In addition to the fundamental plots that are discussed in this chapter, there are other plots available in the Matplotlib package such as contour plots, stream plots, 3D plots, etc., that can be used based on the nature of data or the requirement for analysis. Other than the Matplotlib package, other packages available provide more sophisticated plots that can be used to enhance the visualization for different categories of data. One such package is the Seaborn library, which can be used for making statistical graphics in Python. The Seaborn library provides more sophisticated plots like the boxplot, heatmap, violin plot, cluster map, etc., that can provide enhanced visualization of data. You are encouraged to explore these other categories of plots and libraries.

CHAPTER 7

Analyzing the Data

Exploratory Data Analysis

Exploratory data analysis (EDA) is the process of understanding the data by summarizing its characteristics. This step is important before modeling the data for machine learning. From this analysis, the user can extract the information, identify the root cause of any issues in the data, and figure out the steps to initiate any policies for development. In simple terms, this type of analysis explores the data to understand and identify the patterns and trends in it. There is no common method for doing EDA; it depends on the data we are working with. For simplicity in this chapter, we will use common methods and plots for doing EDA.

Choosing a Dataset

To do the EDA, we'll use the Boston housing dataset that can be imported from the Scikit-Learn library. This dataset was already described in Chapter 6. This dataset contains 506 samples under 13 different feature attributes such as per capita crime rate by town (CRIM), average number of rooms per dwelling (RM), index of accessibility to radial highways (RAD), etc., and a target attribute MEDV indicates the median value of owner-occupied homes in the thousands.

© K. Mohaideen Abdul Kadhar and G. Anand 2021
K. M. Abdul Kadhar and G. Anand, *Data Science with Raspberry Pi*,
https://doi.org/10.1007/978-1-4842-6825-4_7

1. **Import the required libraries.**

   The first step is to load the required libraries for doing the EDA. In this chapter, we will use the packages such as Pandas, NumPy, and Matplotlib for plotting:

   ```
   import matplotlib.pyplot as plt
   import numpy as np
   from sklearn.datasets import load_boston
   ```

2. **Import a dataset.**

   The Boston housing dataset can be imported from the Scikit-Learn library and saved as the boston_data variable, as given in the following code:

   ```
   dataset = load_boston()
   ```

   The more important thing is that most of the open source data is stored in a comma-separated format. This comma-separated format has difficulties fetching and analyzing the data. Thus, the comma-separated data can be converted into a dataframe using the Pandas package in Python.

   ```
   import pandas as pd
   boston_data=pd.DataFrame(dataset.data,columns=dataset.
   feature_names)
   ```

   If the dataset is very large, we can display the top and bottom five rows with headings using the following code:

```
# To display top 5 rows of data
print(boston_data.head(5))
    CRIM   ZN  INDUS  CHAS   NOX   ...  RAD   TAX  PTRATIO   B    LSTAT
0  0.00632 18.0 2.31  0.0  0.538   ...  1.0  296.0  15.3  396.90  4.98
1  0.02731  0.0 7.07  0.0  0.469   ...  2.0  242.0  17.8  396.90  9.14
2  0.02729  0.0 7.07  0.0  0.469   ...  2.0  242.0  17.8  392.83  4.03
3  0.03237  0.0 2.18  0.0  0.458   ...  3.0  222.0  18.7  394.63  2.94
4  0.06905  0.0 2.18  0.0  0.458   ...  3.0  222.0  18.7  396.90  5.33
# To display bottom 5 rows of data
print(boston_data.tail(5))
      CRIM   ZN  INDUS  CHAS   NOX  ...  RAD   TAX  PTRATIO   B    LSTAT
501  0.06263  0.0 11.93  0.0  0.573 ...  1.0  273.0  21.0  391.99  9.67
502  0.04527  0.0 11.93  0.0  0.573 ...  1.0  273.0  21.0  396.90  9.08
503  0.06076  0.0 11.93  0.0  0.573 ...  1.0  273.0  21.0  396.90  5.64
504  0.10959  0.0 11.93  0.0  0.573 ...  1.0  273.0  21.0  393.45  6.48
505  0.04741  0.0 11.93  0.0  0.573 ...  1.0  273.0  21.0  396.90  7.88
```

3. **Check the information about the data in a dataset.**

   Before doing data analysis, checking the information such as the data type and size of the data, describing the data, and knowing the amount of data available in a dataset are important steps because sometimes the numerical values in the dataset may be stored as string data types. It is difficult to plot and analyze numerical values stored as the string data type, so the string data type that is numerical should be converted into integers for better analysis. The size of the dataset can be viewed with the help of the following code:

   ```
   boston_data.shape
   Output:
       (506, 13)
   ```

This output shows that the dataset has 506 rows and 13 columns. In other words, we can say that the dataset has 506 samples with 13 features.

Then, the information about the dataset can be viewed with the help of the following code:

```
boston_data.info()
Output:
<class 'pandas.core.frame.DataFrame'>
RangeIndex: 506 entries, 0 to 505
Data columns (total 13 columns):
 #   Column   Count    Non-Null     Dtype

---  ------            --------------  -----
 0   CRIM       506    non-null     float64
 1   ZN         506    non-null     float64
 2   INDUS      506    non-null     float64
 3   CHAS       506    non-null     float64
 4   NOX        506    non-null     float64
 5   RM         506    non-null     float64
 6   AGE        506    non-null     float64
 7   DIS        506    non-null     float64
 8   RAD        506    non-null     float64
 9   TAX        506    non-null     float64
 10  PTRATIO    506    non-null     float64
 11  B          506    non-null     float64
 12  LSTAT      506    non-null     float64
dtypes: float64(13)
memory usage: 51.5 KB
boston_data.dtypes
Output:
CRIM         float64
ZN           float64
INDUS        float64
```

```
CHAS        float64
NOX         float64
RM          float64
AGE         float64
DIS         float64
RAD         float64
TAX         float64
PTRATIO     float64
B           float64
LSTAT       float64
dtype:      object
```

Moreover, with the help of describe() function, we can see the distribution of data such as minimum values, maximum values, mean, etc. The description of the Boston data can be viewed using the following code:

```
boston_data.describe()
Output:
```

	CRIM	ZN	INDUS	...	PTRATIO
B	LSTAT				
count	506.000000	506.000000	506.000000	...	506.000000
506.000000	506.000000				
mean	3.613524	11.363636	11.136779	...	18.455534
356.674032	12.653063				
std	8.601545	23.322453	6.860353	...	2.164946
91.294864	7.141062				
min	0.006320	0.000000	0.460000	...	12.600000
0.320000	1.730000				
25 percent	0.082045	0.000000	5.190000	...	17.400000
375.377500	6.950000				
50 percent	0.256510	0.000000	9.690000	...	19.050000
391.440000	11.360000				

```
75 percent   3.677083      12.500000   18.100000    ...   20.200000
396.225000   16.955000
max          88.976200    100.000000   27.740000    ...   22.000000
396.900000   37.970000
```

Modifying the Columns in the Dataset

Modifications in the data such as removing unnecessary columns, adding dummy columns, dropping duplicate columns, encoding the column, and normalizing the data are required if the dataset needs to have preprocessing done. Dropping the unnecessary columns is more important when many columns are not used for analysis. Dropping those columns is the better solution to make the data lighter and reliable. Dropping the unnecessary columns in the Boston dataset can be done with the following code:

```
boston_data =boston_data.drop(['CRIM','ZN','LSTAT'])
print(boston_data.head(5))
Output:
     INDUS CHAS NOX     RM     AGE   DIS     RAD  TAX    PTRATIO  B
  0  2.31  0.0  0.538  6.575  65.2  4.0900  1.0  296.0  15.3   396.90
  1  7.07  0.0  0.469  6.421  78.9  4.9671  2.0  242.0  17.8   396.90
  2  7.07  0.0  0.469  7.185  61.1  4.9671  2.0  242.0  17.8   392.83
  3  2.18  0.0  0.458  6.998  45.8  6.0622  3.0  222.0  18.7   394.63
  4  2.18  0.0  0.458  7.147  54.2  6.0622  3.0  222.0  18.7   396.90
```

In the previous code, the columns of CRIM, ZN, and LSTAT are dropped, and only 10 columns of data are presented.

Renaming the column name helps the user to improve the readability of the data. In the following code, the column name DIS is renamed to Distance:

```
boston_data= boston_data.rename(columns={"DIS":"Distance"})
boston_data.head(5)
```

	INDUS	CHAS	NOX	RM	AGE	Distance	RAD	TAX	PTRATIO	B
0	2.31	0.0	0.538	6.575	65.2	4.0900	1.0	296.0	15.3	396.90
1	7.07	0.0	0.469	6.421	78.9	4.9671	2.0	242.0	17.8	396.90
2	7.07	0.0	0.469	7.185	61.1	4.9671	2.0	242.0	17.8	392.83
3	2.18	0.0	0.458	6.998	45.8	6.0622	3.0	222.0	18.7	394.63
4	2.18	0.0	0.458	7.147	54.2	6.0622	3.0	222.0	18.7	396.90

Identifying duplicates, dropping the duplicates, and detecting outliers were already discussed in the previous chapters.

Statistical Analysis

A better understanding of the data at hand can go a long way in simplifying the job of a data scientist, and this is where statistics can come in handy. Statistics can provide the tools necessary to identify structures in the data, and such insights can prove to be valuable in building a model to best fit our data. The role of statistics with respect to data can vary from simple analysis to creating self-learning models. In this section, we will introduce the various types of distributions, statistical measures of data, and ways to fit data to distributions.

Before discussing distributions, let's first understand how data is associated with probability. When we consider a dataset, it normally represents a single sample from a population. For instance, if we have a dataset consisting of the height and weight of all the students in a school, the model developed from this data after some statistical analysis can be used to predict the height and weight of students from another school. The dataset in our hand is just one sample, whereas the population may consist of as many schools.

The numerical data that we encounter may be continuous or discrete in nature. The difference between the two is that the continuous data may take any value, whereas the discrete data can take only certain values. For example, data such as the number of cars manufactured per day, the number of feedback received from customers, etc., are discrete in nature, whereas data such as height, weight, humidity, temperature, etc., represents continuous data.

Probability distributions, a fundamental concept in statistics, provide a way to represent the possible values taken by a random variable and the respective probabilities. The *probability mass function* (PMF) denotes the discrete probability distribution, and the *probability density function* (PDF) denotes the continuous probability distribution. Some of the common distributions that a data scientist needs to be aware of are discussed in the following section.

Uniform Distribution

Uniform distribution, also called a *rectangular distribution*, has a constant probability. In other words, all the outcomes have the same probability of occurrence. The number of outcomes in the case of uniform distribution may be unlimited. The most common example for a uniform distribution is the roll of a fair die, where all six outcomes have an equal probability of 1/6. Let's illustrate uniform distribution by plotting the probabilities of the outcomes for the fair die experiment. In other words, the probabilities of occurrence for each face of the die are equally likely. Figure 7-1 shows the distribution plot.

```
import numpy as np
import matplotlib.pyplot as plt
probabilities = np.full((6),1/6)
events = [1,2,3,4,5,6]
plt.bar(events,probabilities)
plt.xlabel('Die roll events')
plt.ylabel('Event Probability')
plt.title('Fair die - Uniform Distribution')
plt.show()
```

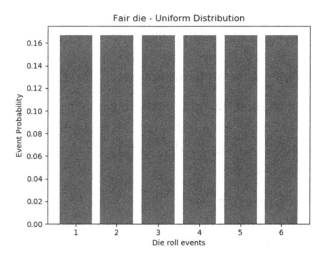

Figure 7-1. *Uniform distribution of fair die experiment*

If a histogram plot is made for a dataset by dividing the numerical data into a number of bins and all the bins are found to have equal distribution, then the dataset can be said to be uniformly distributed.

Binomial Distribution

As the name suggests, this distribution is used when there are only two possible outcomes. A random variable X that follows a binomial distribution is dependent on two parameters:

- The number of trials n in the case of binomial distribution must be fixed, and the trials are considered to be independent of each other. In other words, the outcome of a particular trial does not depend on the outcomes of the previous trials.

- There are only two possible outcomes for each event: success or failure. The probability of success, say p, remains the same from trial to trial.

Therefore, the binomial distribution function in Python normally takes two values as inputs: the number of trials n and the probability of success p. To understand binomial distribution, let's look at the common experiment of tossing a coin:

```
from scipy.stats import binom
import matplotlib.pyplot as plt
import numpy as np
n=15 # no of times coin is tossed
r_values = list(range(n + 1))
x=[0.2,0.5,0.7,0.9]  #probabilities of getting a head
k=1
for p in x:
    dist = [binom.pmf(r, n, p) for r in r_values ]
    plt.subplot(2,2,k)
    plt.bar(r_values,dist)
    plt.xlabel('number of heads')
```

```
    plt.ylabel('probability')
    plt.title('p= percent.1f' percentp)
    k+=1
plt.show()
```

In the previous code, we have 15 trials for tossing the coin. The probability of getting a head remains the same for each trial, and the outcome of each trial is independent of the previous outcomes. The binomial distribution is computed using the `binom.pmf` function available in the `stats` module of the `scipy` package. The experiment is repeated for different probabilities of success using a `for` loop, and Figure 7-2 shows the resulting distribution plot.

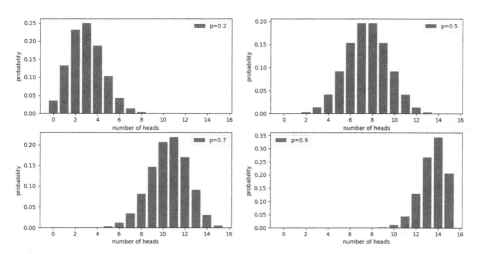

Figure 7-2. *Binomial distribution for tossing a coin 15 times*

Figure 7-2 shows the binomial distribution for our coin toss experiment for different probabilities of success. The first subplot shows the binomial distribution when the probability of getting a head is 0.2. This implies that there is a 20 percent chance of getting a head. Twenty percent of 15 tosses is 3, which implies that there is a high probability of getting three heads in 15 tosses. Hence, the probability is at a maximum of 3.

It can be seen that the binomial distribution has a bell-shaped response. The response is skewed to the left when the probability of success is low and shifts to the right with an increase in probability, as illustrated in the rest of the subplots.

Binomial distribution can be encountered in various domains of data science. For instance, when a pharmaceutical company wants to test a new vaccine, then there are only two possible outcomes: the vaccine works or it does not. Also, the result for an individual patient is an independent event and does not depend on other trials for different patients. Binomial distribution can be applied to various business issues as well. For example, consider people working in the sales department making calls all day to sell their company's products. The outcome of the call is whether a successful sale is made or not, and the outcome is independent for each worker. Similarly, there are many other areas in a business with binary outcomes where binomial distribution can be applied, and hence it plays an important role in business decision-making.

Normal Distribution

Normal distribution, also known as Gaussian distribution, is normally a bell-shaped curve centered at the mean where the probability is the maximum, and the probability reduces the further we move from the mean. This implies that the values closer to the mean occur more frequently, and the values that are further away from the mean occur less frequently. This distribution is dependent on two parameters: the mean (μ) of the data and the standard deviation (σ). The probability density function (pdf) for a normal distribution can be given as follows:

$$f(x; \mu, \sigma) = \frac{1}{\sqrt{2\pi\sigma^2}} e^{-\frac{(x-\mu)^2}{2\sigma^2}}$$

To illustrate the pdf function, consider the following code. An array x with 100 values in the range of -10 to 10 is created, and the pdf function of x is computed using the norm.pdf function in the stats module of the scipy package. The pdf function is computed for four different values of mean 0, 2.5, 5, and 7.5 using a for loop. If the mean value is not given, the norm.pdf function takes a default value of zero.

```python
from scipy.stats import norm
import matplotlib.pyplot as plt
import numpy as np
mean=[0.0,2.5,5,7.5] # mean values for the normal distribution
x=np.linspace(-10,10,100) # array of 100 numbers in the
range -10 to 10
for m in mean:
    y=norm.pdf(x,loc=m)
    plt.plot(x,y,label='mean= %.1f' %m)
plt.xlabel('x')
plt.ylabel('pdf(x)')
plt.legend(frameon=True)
plt.show()
```

Figure 7-3 shows that the normal distribution produces a bell-shaped curve that is centered on the mean value. That is, the curve is at the maximum at the point of mean, and it starts decreasing on either side as we move away from the mean value. Note that we have not specified the value of standard deviation. In that case, the norm.pdf function takes the default value of 1.

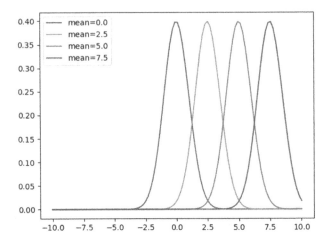

Figure 7-3. *Normal distribution plot for different mean values*

Similarly, let's keep the value of the mean as constant and plot the distribution for different values of standard distribution using the following code:

```
from scipy.stats import norm
import matplotlib.pyplot as plt
import numpy as np
stdev=[1.0,2.0,3.0,4.0] # standard deviation values for the
normal distribution
x=np.linspace(-10,10,100)
for s in stdev:
            y=norm.pdf(x,scale=s)
            plt.plot(x,y,label='stdev= %.1f' %s)
plt.xlabel('x')
plt.ylabel('pdf(x)')
plt.legend(frameon=True)
plt.show()
```

From Figure 7-4, we can see that all four curves are centered at the default mean value of zero. As the value of standard deviation σ is increased, the density is distributed across a wide range. In other words, the distribution of data is more spread out from the mean as the standard deviation value is increased and there is a high likelihood that more observations are further away from the mean.

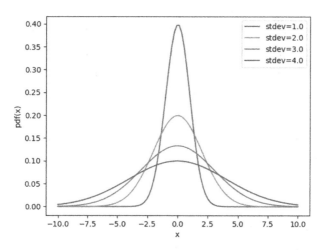

Figure 7-4. *Normal distribution plot for different values of standard deviation*

An important property of the normal distribution that makes it an important statistical distribution for data scientists is the *empirical rule.* According to this rule, if we divide the range of observations in the x-axis in terms of standard deviation, then approximately 68.3 percent of the values fall within one standard deviation from the mean, 95.5 percent of the values fall within two standard deviation, and 99.7 percent of the values fall within three standard deviations, respectively. This empirical rule can be used for identifying outliers in the data if the data can be fit to a normal distribution. This principle is used in the Z-score for outlier detection, which we discussed earlier in Chapter 5.

Statistical Analysis of Boston Housing Price Dataset

Let's take the Boston housing price dataset and try to identify the best features that can be used to model the data based on the statistical properties of the features. As we have already discussed, the Boston dataset consists of 13 different features for 506 cases (506 × 13). In addition to these features, the median value of owner-occupied homes (in the thousands) denoted by the variable MEDV is identified as the target. That is, given the 13 different features, the median value of a house is to be estimated. The features from the dataset are first converted to a dataframe using the Pandas package. Then the target variable is added to the last column of this dataframe, making its dimension 506 × 14. This is illustrated in the following code:

```
import matplotlib.pyplot as plt
import numpy as np
import pandas as pd
from sklearn.datasets import load_boston
import matplotlib.pyplot as plt
dataset = load_boston()
boston_data=pd.DataFrame(dataset.data,columns=dataset.feature_
names)
boston_data['MEDV'] = dataset['target']
print(boston_data.head())
```

```
    CRIM      ZN    INDUS  CHAS  NOX    ...  TAX    PTRATIO  B
LSTAT   MEDV
0   0.00632  18.0   2.31   0.0   0.538  ...  296.0  15.3    396.90
4.98    24.0
1   0.02731   0.0   7.07   0.0   0.469  ...  242.0  17.8    396.90
9.14    21.6
2   0.02729   0.0   7.07   0.0   0.469  ...  242.0  17.8    392.83
4.03    34.7
3   0.03237   0.0   2.18   0.0   0.458  ...  222.0  18.7    394.63
2.94    33.4
4   0.06905   0.0   2.18   0.0   0.458  ...  222.0  18.7    396.90
5.33    36.2
[5 rows x 14 columns]
```

Once we have the data in hand, the best way to go about it is to plot the histogram of all the features so that we can get an understanding of the nature of their distribution. Rather than plotting the histogram of each feature individually, the hist function in the Pandas package can be used to plot them all in one go, as illustrated here:

```
fig, axis = plt.subplots(2,7,figsize=(16, 16))
boston_data.hist(ax=axis,grid=False)
plt.show()
```

From Figure 7-5, we can see that the distribution of the target variable MEDV is like a normal distribution.

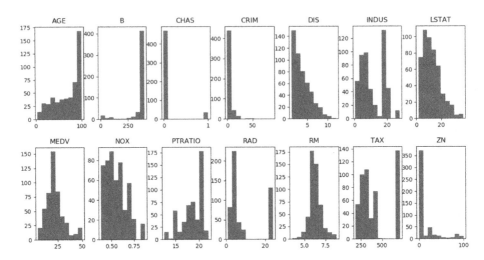

Figure 7-5. *Histogram plots of the Boston dataset features*

Further, if we observe all the other parameters, the distribution for the parameter RM (which denotes the average number of rooms per dwelling) is also similar to the target MEDV. Therefore, the RM can definitely be used for modeling the dataset. Also, the parameters DIS (weighted mean of distances to five Boston employment centers) and LSTAT (percentage of lower status of the population) have similar distribution. The distribution of the parameter AGE (proportion of owner-occupied units built prior to 1940) is exactly the opposite of these two parameters. The rest of the parameters have less significant distribution compared to the target parameter. Since these three parameters seem to be related either positively or negatively, it is pointless to use all three for building the model. So, we have to see which of these three parameters are related to our target variable MEDV. The best way to do this is to measure the correlation between these parameters using the corr function in the Pandas package, as illustrated here:

```
cols=['RM','AGE','DIS','LSTAT','MEDV']
print(boston_data[cols].corr())
```

	RM	AGE	DIS	LSTAT	MEDV
RM	1.000000	-0.240265	0.205246	-0.613808	0.695360
AGE	-0.240265	1.000000	-0.747881	0.602339	-0.376955
DIS	0.205246	-0.747881	1.000000	-0.496996	0.249929
LSTAT	-0.613808	0.602339	-0.496996	1.000000	-0.737663
MEDV	0.695360	-0.376955	0.249929	-0.737663	1.000000

From these results, it can be seen that the diagonal elements are all 1s, which implies maximum correlation, and they represent the self-correlation values. If we look at the row corresponding to our target parameter MEDV, we can see that RM is positively more correlated with MEDV as we judged earlier looking at the histogram distribution. It can be also seen that the parameter LSTAT is negatively more correlated with MEDV, which implies that there will be an inverse relationship between these two parameters. A scatter plot of RM and LSTAT against MEDV, respectively, would give us a better understanding of this relationship, as illustrated here:

```
plt.subplot(1,2,1)
plt.scatter(list(boston_data['RM']),list(boston_data['MEDV']))
plt.xlabel('RM')
plt.ylabel('MEDV')
plt.subplot(1,2,2)
plt.scatter(list(boston_data['LSTAT']),list(boston_
data['MEDV']))
plt.xlabel('LSTAT')
plt.ylabel('MEDV')
plt.show()
```

Figure 7-6 confirms our conclusions derived using the distribution graphs and the correlation values. It can be seen that RM and MEDV are positively correlated; i.e., the median value of owner-occupied homes increases with an increase in the average number of rooms per dwelling. Similarly, it can be seen that LSTAT and MEDV are negatively correlated; i.e., the median value of the owner-occupied home drops with an increase in the percentage of a lower status of population. Therefore, these two parameters are good choices to model the Boston housing dataset. It can also be seen from the figure that there are some outliers in the RM versus MEDV plot, which could be treated using the techniques discussed in Chapter 5 before further processing.

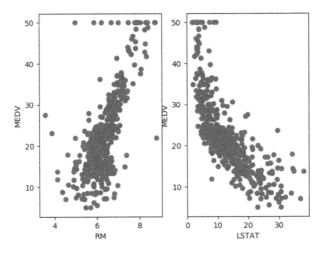

Figure 7-6. *Scatter plot of RM and LSTAT versus MEDV*

CHAPTER 8

Learning from Data

Learning from data just means extracting the information from the data and using it for predicting/forecasting in order to make intelligent decisions based on it. This area is becoming more popular because it is applicable to various applications in different industries, such as financial, healthcare, education, computer vision, politics, etc.

Learning from data is used in various situations when the analytical solution is not required or there is no clear-cut model about the problem or requirement of forecasting based on the previous information, etc. Basically, three types of learning techniques are available: supervised learning, unsupervised learning, and reinforcement learning. *Supervised learning* utilizes the observations of a process to develop a model. Supervised learning models are trained based on the input and output observations (i.e., input and output data) of the process. In *unsupervised learning*, the training data doesn't have any information about the output. The unsupervised models categorize the model based on the characteristics of the data. Also, unsupervised models can be used to find patterns in the data, detect outliers by clustering similar data, find the structure of the data, etc. The *reinforcement learning* model also doesn't utilize the correct information about the output. However, it has some possible output with information about the quality of the output.

K. M. Abdul Kadhar and G. Anand, *Data Science with Raspberry Pi*,
https://doi.org/10.1007/978-1-4842-6825-4_8

This chapter focuses on describing the learning model development techniques by utilizing the Boston dataset. Then, we will implement the learning models in the Raspberry Pi and analyze the industry data that is acquired from the sensors. This implementation will be discussed as a case study in Chapter 9.

Forecasting from Data Using Regression

Regression finds the relationship between the variables in a dataset. Regression is used to identify the impact of one variable on another variable. Also, it can be used to forecast a variable based on its previous data. Regression models can be used in many areas such as forecasting the trends in economics, predicting sales in business, predicting the impact of some policies, and predicting the blood pressure levels in healthcare applications.

In regression, there are two kinds of variables required to develop a model: input and output. An *input variable* is the variable in a dataset used to predict the output variable. An input variable in linear regression is commonly denoted as X. An *output variable* is the variable for predicting and is denoted as Y. Equation 8-1 shows the equation for linear regression.

$$Ye = \alpha + \beta X \qquad \ldots (8\text{-}1)$$

Here, Ye is the estimated output variable, Y is the actual output variable, and α and β are parameters of the linear regression model. For example, if we want to buy a TV and try to estimate the cost of the TV (i.e., output variable), we use input variables like the size of the TV. Now, α, β, and Y are selected (randomly) as 2, 5, and €170, respectively. The size of the TV (i.e., input variable) is 32 inch, and the estimated output of the linear regression model in estimating the cost of the TV is shown in Equation 8-2.

$$Ye=2+5 *32$$

$$= €162 \qquad ...(8\text{-}2)$$

So, based on Equation 8-2, the cost of the TV is €162 when the size of the TV is 32 inches, which is nearer to the actual cost of the TV: €170. If we modify the parameters α and β as 0.1 and 0.5, respectively, now the estimated cost of the TV is calculated as follows:

$$Ye=0.1+0.5 *32$$

$$= €16.1$$

The cost of the TV is drastically changed to €16.1. This shows that the selection of α and β is important in predicting the output variable. Thus, the objective in developing the linear regression model is to find α and β by minimizing the difference between the actual output Y and the estimated output Ye. There are many methods available to find the optimum parameters of α and β. However, the ordinary least (OL) square method is commonly used in finding the optimum parameters of α and β.

The OL method uses covariance and variance of the input variables for identifying the parameters α and β as shown in Equation 8-3.

$$\beta = \frac{Cov(X,Y)}{Var(X)}$$
$$\alpha = \bar{Y} - \beta\bar{X} \qquad ... (8\text{-}3)$$

Here, $\bar{Y}$ and $\bar{X}$ are the means of actual output and input variables.

Let's consider the Boston dataset now. The RM variable is used for representing the average number of rooms per dwelling, and the target variable (i.e., output variable) MEDV is used for representing the median value of owner-occupied homes in the thousands. We consider RM as the input variable and MEDV as the output variable for linear regression modeling. Because RM and MEDV are interlinked with each other closely, the linear regression model for those variables can be implemented using the following code. For identifying the α and β parameters, the ordinary least square method is used.

```
from sklearn.linear_model import LinearRegression
import matplotlib.pyplot as plt
import numpy as np
from sklearn.datasets import load_boston
import pandas as pd
dataset = load_boston()
boston_data=pd.DataFrame(dataset.data,columns=dataset.feature_
names)
Target=pd.DataFrame(dataset.target,columns=['target'])
# two variable for regression model
X1=boston_data['RM']
X=X1.to_numpy()  # dataframe is converted in to array for
arithmetic operations
Y=dataset.target
xmean=np.mean(X)
ymean=np.mean(Y)
xcov=np.multiply((X-xmean),(Y-ymean))
xvar=(X-xmean)**2
# linear regression model
beta=xcov.sum()/xvar.sum()
alpha=ymean-(beta*xmean)
print(beta)
print(alpha)
```

The output of α and β values from the OLS method is shown here:

```
Beta value is 9.10210898118031
Alpha value is -34.67062077643857
```

The linear regression model can be developed by using the previous α and β values, as given in Equation 8-4.

$$Ye=-34.6706+9.1021*X \qquad \dots (8\text{-}4)$$

Here, X is the input variable RM. It can be implemented using the following code:

```
# prediction model
ye=alpha+beta*X
```

Let's plot the actual output variable Y and the estimated model Ye, which gives clear insight about their relationships and can be plotted using the following code (see Figure 8-1):

```
# plot
plt.figure(figsize=(12,6))
plt.plot(X1,ye)
plt.plot(X,Y,'ro')
plt.title('Actual Vs Predicted')
plt.xlabel('X')
plt.ylabel('Y')
plt.show()
```

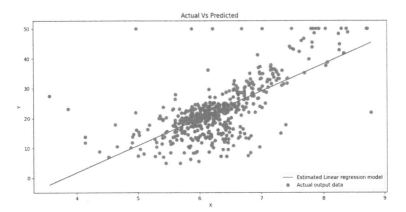

Figure 8-1. *Actual output variable versus estimated linear regression model*

Linear Regression using Scikit-Learn

In the previous example, a linear regression predictor uses one input variable for predicting the output. The output can be predicted with more than one variable based on the given linear regression (see Equation 8-5).

$$Ye = \alpha + \beta_1 x_1 + \beta_2 x_2 + \beta_3 x_3 + \ldots\ldots + \beta_n x_n \qquad \ldots\ldots(8\text{-}5)$$

Equation 8-5 used n number of input variables for predicting the output variable Ye. If we consider all the input variables of the Boston dataset (totally 13 input variables) and output variables (MEDV), the regression model by using multiple variables can be implemented using Scikit-Learn and is given in the following code:

```
from sklearn.linear_model import LinearRegression
import matplotlib.pyplot as plt
import numpy as np
import seaborn as sns
from sklearn.datasets import load_boston
import pandas as pd
dataset = load_boston()
```

```
boston_data=pd.DataFrame(dataset.data,columns=dataset.feature_
names)
Target=pd.DataFrame(dataset.target,columns=['target'])
# two variable for regression model
X=boston_data
Y=Target
lm=LinearRegression()
model=lm.fit(X,Y)
print(f'alpha={model.intercept_}')
print(f'beta={model.coef_}')
Ye=model.predict(X)
Y1=Y.to_numpy()
E=np.mean(Y1-Ye)
MSE=E**2
print(MSE)
# plot
plt.figure(figsize=(12,6))
plt.scatter(Y1,np.arange(0,len(Y)),color='red')
plt.title('Actual')
plt.xlabel('No of samples')
plt.ylabel('Y')
#plt.figure(figsize=(12,6))
plt.scatter(Ye,np.arange(0,len(Y)),color='blue')
plt.legend(['Actual output data','Estimated Linear regression
model', ])
plt.show()
```

Output:

For α and β values

```
    alpha=[36.45948839]
    beta=[[-1.08011358e-01  4.64204584e-02  2.05586264e-02
    2.68673382e+00
```

```
-1.77666112e+01   3.80986521e+00   6.92224640e-04 -
    1.47556685e+00
  3.06049479e-01 -1.23345939e-02 -9.52747232e-01
      9.31168327e-03
-5.24758378e-01]]
```

To evaluate the quality of the model, we can use the mean square error (MSE) metric. MSE finds the average of the squared error between the actual output and the predicted output.

```
1.8463848451630152e-29
```

Figure 8-2 compares the actual output (Y) to the predicted output (Ye).

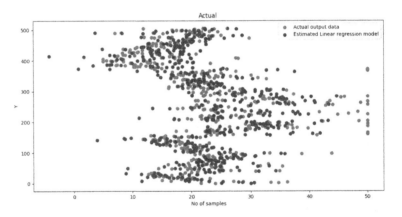

Figure 8-2. *Actual output data to the predicted output data using linear regression*

Principal Component Analysis

Principal component analysis is a statistical method used to extract the strong features in a large dataset. In other words, the dimension of the dataset can be reduced by extracting the important features from the dataset. PCA uses standardization for identifying the distances between the features and implements the covariance information for identifying

162

any relationship between the features. Then, with the help of the eigenvectors and eigenvalues, the principal components are calculated. The principal components are used to extract the strong features, i.e., reduce the dimensionality of the data. Further, the principal components are used to optimize the number of clusters for the k-means clustering technique, and the Boston dataset is used for this work. The Boston dataset has 13 features. In the first step, the strong features in the Boston dataset are identified with the help of PCA using the following code:

```
from sklearn.decomposition import PCA
from sklearn.preprocessing import StandardScaler
#config InlineBackend.figure_format='retina'
# Load in the data
from sklearn.datasets import load_boston
dataset = load_boston()
df=pd.DataFrame(dataset.data,columns=dataset.feature_names)
#df = pd.read_csv('2013_2014_cleaned.csv')
# Standardize the data to have a mean of ~0 and a variance of 1
X_std = StandardScaler().fit_transform(df)
# Create a PCA instance: pca
pca = PCA(n_components=13)
principalComponents = pca.fit_transform(X_std)
# Plot the explained variances
features = range(pca.n_components_)
plt.bar(features, pca.explained_variance_ratio_, color='black')
plt.xlabel('PCA features')
plt.ylabel('variance %')
plt.xticks(features)
plt.show()
# Save components to a DataFrame
PCA_components = pd.DataFrame(principalComponents)
```

From Figure 8-3, we can see that the first three features give a good variance in the dataset.

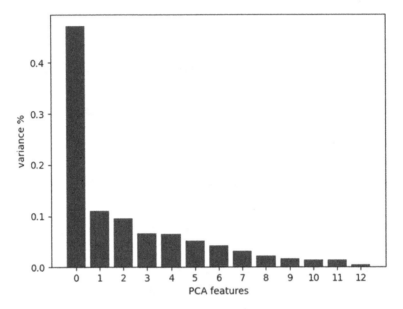

Figure 8-3. *Features in the dataset with respect to variance*

Hence, five features can be selected for clustering. For clustering, k-means clustering can be used. To identify the optimal number of clusters, the PCA is fit with the k-means clustering algorithms and calculates the inertia of the clustering model with the selected principal components. The following code identifies the inertia of the clustering model and plots the number of clusters (i.e., k) with the inertia (this code continues with the previous PCA code). Figure 8-4 shows the plot of inertia against the number of clusters (k). From Figure 8-4, it can be concluded that after the number of cluster (k = 5), there are no significant changes occurring in the inertia. Hence, five can be chosen as the optimal number of cluster heads for the given dataset.

```
ks = range(1, 10)
inertias = []
for k in ks:
    # Create a KMeans instance with k clusters: model
    model = KMeans(n_clusters=k)

    # Fit model to samples
    model.fit(PCA_components.iloc[:,:3])

    # Append the inertia to the list of inertias
    inertias.append(model.inertia_)

plt.plot(ks, inertias, '-*', color='blue')
plt.xlabel('number of clusters, k')
plt.ylabel('inertia')
plt.xticks(ks)
plt.show()
```

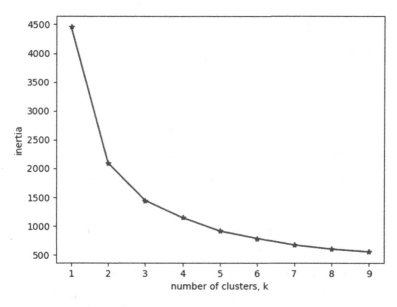

Figure 8-4. *Number of clusters versus inertia*

Outlier Detection Using K-Means Clustering

Clustering is an exploratory data analysis technique used in unsupervised learning problems, i.e., when there is no prior knowledge about the data. The idea behind clustering is to group the data points in a dataset into a number of subgroups called *clusters*. The data points in each cluster are more similar to the other points in the same cluster than those of other clusters.

The technique that is used widely for clustering operations is the centroid-based method called *k-means clustering*, which is an iterative algorithm that splits the dataset into k nonoverlapping clusters where each data point is assigned to only one cluster. The condition for assigning data points to a cluster is that the sum of the squared overlapping clusters' distance of the data points to the cluster's centroid is at a minimum. The k-means algorithm works as follows:

1. Specify the number of clusters.

2. Randomly select center points for each cluster, also called *centroids*.

3. Calculate the distance between each data point and the cluster centroids, and assign the points to the cluster whose distance is minimum.

4. Recompute the centroid for each cluster by taking the average of all the data points assigned to the cluster.

5. Iterate steps 3 and 4 until there is no change to the centroids.

In addition to clustering the data, the k-means algorithm can be used to identify outliers present in the data. The idea behind this approach is to sort the distances from each data point to the cluster centroid in ascending order and treat a portion of the data points that have the maximum distance from the centroid as outliers.

To illustrate this approach, let's look at the Boston housing dataset. As we discussed in Chapter 7, the average number of rooms per dwelling (RM) and the medium value of owner-occupied homes in the thousands (MEDV) are highly correlated. So, these two parameters are taken as two-dimensional data for the clustering algorithm, as illustrated in the following code:

```
import matplotlib.pyplot as plt
import numpy as np
import pandas as pd
from sklearn.cluster import KMeans
from sklearn.preprocessing import scale
from numpy import sqrt, random, array, argsort
from sklearn.datasets import load_boston
dataset = load_boston()
boston_data=pd.DataFrame(dataset.data,columns=dataset.feature_
names)
x=boston_data['RM']
y=dataset.target
x=x.to_numpy() # convert pandas series data to numpy array
x=x.reshape(x.shape[0],1)
x=scale(x)
y=y.reshape(y.shape[0],1)
y=scale(y)
X=np.zeros((np.shape(x)[0],2))
X[:,0]=x[:,0]
X[:,1]=y[:,0]
```

The features of the dataset are first loaded to a dataframe. The column corresponding to the feature RM is moved from the dataframe to the variable x. Since the RM feature stored in variable x is in the Pandas series format, it is converted to a NumPy array using the to_numpy function, making it viable for applying the k-means algorithm. This array is then reshaped as it has to be stored along with the target variable MEDV in a two-dimensional array. Then an additional scaling of the parameter is done by using the scale function in the sklearn package. This is done to normalize the data within a particular range. In a similar fashion, the target MEDV feature (which by default is a NumPy array) is also stored in the variable y, reshaped and scaled. The two variables x and y are then combined in the variable X thereby making it a two-dimensional variable. The application of k-means algorithm to this variable is illustrated in the following code:

```
km=KMeans(n_clusters=1).fit(X)
distance = km.transform(X)
indexes = np.argsort(distance.ravel())[::-1][:20]
```

The Kmeans function imported from the sklearn package can be used to implement the clustering algorithm. This function can take inputs such as the number of clusters, the maximum number of iterations, and more. In our code, we are giving an input of one for number of clusters. In other words, we are going to group all the data points into a single cluster. Since the maximum number of iterations is not specified, the default value of 300 iterations is taken by the function. After fitting the k-means algorithm to our data, the next step is to compute the distance of each data point from the cluster centroid. This is done using the transform function in the sklearn package. The resulting distance variable is also an n-dimensional NumPy array. Therefore, it is first flattened using the ravel function, and then the flattened array is sorted in descending order. This means the array starts with the data points that are further from the cluster center and ends with the points that are closer to the center. This sorting is done using the argsort function, which provides the indexes corresponding to the sorted data points.

We know that outliers are abnormal data points that lie far away from the other data points in the dataset. But what is considered abnormal is left to the analyst who is aware of the requirements of the analysis. In the case of the Boston housing data, the outliers are the high median value for homes with fewer rooms (overpriced), the low median value for homes with more rooms (erroneous), and also depending on requirements the median value of the number of room combinations beyond a particular limit. To detect these outliers, we randomly pick the first 20 indexes from the sorted index array and mark the data points corresponding to those indexes in a scatter plot of all data points, as illustrated here:

```
f,ax=plt.subplots()
ax.scatter(X[:,0],X[:,1])
ax.scatter(X[indexes][:,0],X[indexes][:,1],edgecolors='r',
           facecolors='none', s=100)
plt.xlabel('MEDV')
plt.ylabel('RM')
f.show()
```

Figure 8-5 shows a scatter plot of the average number of rooms per dwelling against the median value of owner-occupied homes. The outliers in the data are indicated by those points with red circles around them.

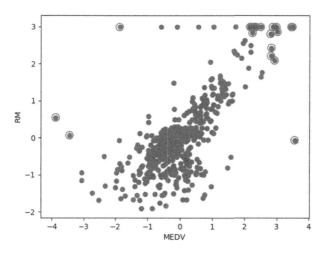

Figure 8-5. *Outliers detected using the k-means clustering algorithm*

CHAPTER 9

Case Studies

This chapter presents real-world case studies for implementing data science concepts. Three scenarios are considered: data science concepts for human emotion classification with EEG signals, image data, and Industry 4.0.

For human emotion classification, EEG signals of humans are extracted using a NeuroSky MindWave Mobile kit, and the EEG signals are received and analyzed in the Raspberry Pi. A NeuroSky MindWave Mobile kit and the Raspberry Pi can be connected via Bluetooth. In image data, data science steps are applied to preprocess the image data for further analysis. In the Industry 4.0 case study, the Raspberry Pi acts as a localized cloud. Here, many sensors are connected to the Raspberry Pi, and the signals from the sensors are converted to structured data for further analysis and visualization.

Case Study 1: Human Emotion Classification

An emotion is a feeling that is characterized by intense brain activity. A considerable amount of research has been focused on recognizing human emotions for a wide range of applications such as medical, health, robotics, and brain-computer interface (BCI) applications. There are a number of ways to recognize human emotions such as facial emotion recognition, tone recognition from speech signal, emotion recognition from EEG signals, etc. Among those, classification from EEG signals is a

© K. Mohaideen Abdul Kadhar and G. Anand 2021
K. M. Abdul Kadhar and G. Anand, *Data Science with Raspberry Pi*,
https://doi.org/10.1007/978-1-4842-6825-4_9

simple and convenient method. Also, EEG signals have useful information about human emotions. Thus, many researchers have focused on classifying human emotion using EEG signals. EEG signals are used to record the human brain activity by measuring electrical signals by placing electrodes on the scalp.

Let's consider a simple emotion recognition system that uses a single electrode device, namely, a NeuroSky MindWave device for acquiring the EEG signals from participants and classifying their emotion as happy, afraid, or sad with the help of machine learning algorithms, namely, k-nearest neighbor (k-NN) and neural networks (NNs).

Methodology

The participants included are from different age groups, and they were subjected to the experiment separately by showing them images in different categories from the worldwide recognized database Geneva Affective Picture Database (GAPED). The images include images of babies, happy scenarios, animal mistreatments, human concerns, snakes, and spiders, each kindling different emotions in the participants. The dataset of features corresponding to the recorded EEG signals is then obtained for all the participants, and these features are then subjected to machine learning models like k-NN and NN, which classifies each signal into one of three emotions: happy, afraid, or sad.

Dataset

The two devices that are used for data collection are the NeuroSky MindWave Mobile device and a Raspberry Pi 3 board. The NeuroSky MindWave device can be used to safely record the EEG signals. The device consists of a headset, an ear clip, and a sensor (electrode) arm. The headset's ground electrodes are available on the ear clip, whereas the EEG electrode is on the sensor arm that will rest on the forehead above the eye after putting on the headset. The device uses a single AAA battery, which can last for eight hours.

This device is connected to a Raspberry Pi 3 board via Bluetooth, as shown in Figure 9-1. It is a third-generation Raspberry Pi model that comes with a quad-core processor, 1GB of RAM, and a number of ports for connecting various devices. It also comes with wireless LAN and Bluetooth support, which can help to connect wireless devices like our MindWave Mobile. The software provided by the NeuroSky device vendor is installed on the Pi board to acquire the serial data from the device.

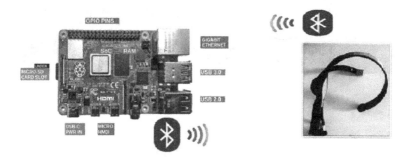

Figure 9-1. *Raspberry Pi with MindWave Mobile connected via Bluetooth*

Interfacing the Raspberry Pi with MindWave Mobile via Bluetooth

There are two ways to connect the MindWave Mobile with the Raspberry Pi. The first one is to connect the MindWave Mobile with the Raspberry Pi desktop. Initially switch on the Raspberry Pi, boot into the Raspberry Pi operating system, and then switch on the MindWave Mobile Bluetooth. Then click the Bluetooth symbol in the Raspberry Pi OS, which will show the devices that are ready to pair with the Raspberry Pi. In the list, the

MindWave Mobile can be selected, and the pairing password 0000 as prescribed by the vendor can be used. Now, the MindWave Mobile device is paired with the Pi, as shown in Figure 9-2.

(a)

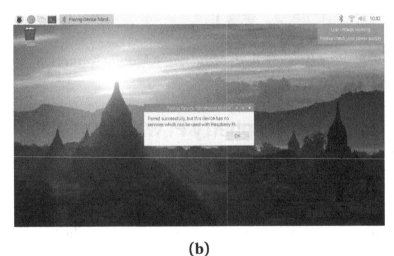

(b)

Figure 9-2. *Raspberry desktop pairing with MindWave Mobile*

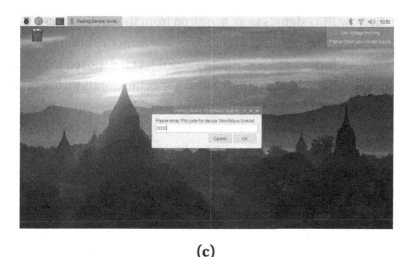

(c)

Figure 9-2. (*continued*)

The signals from the MindWave Mobile device can be extracted via this Bluetooth connection. Another way to connect the Raspberry with MindWave is by using Pypi 0.1.0. The steps are explained at `https://github.com/cttoronto/python-MindWave-mobile`. This link provides the data about alpha, beta, and gamma values of the brainwave signals. However, in this work, the dataset is developed from the EEG signals.

Data Collection Process

The participants are seated in a small, darkened room, which is also radio silent to prevent them from acoustic and visual disturbances. The terms and conditions are explained prior to the experiment, and they are instructed to stop the test if they have any discomfort. A manual score sheet was also provided to the participants to rate their emotions during each picture. There was a total of 15 participants, and 15 signals spread across three different emotions were recorded, thereby making a total of $15 \times 3 = 45$ EEG signals. The emotions were happy, afraid, and sad.

Initially, raw EEG signals were acquired from the user using a NeuroSky device. The raw EEG signal extracted from the brain cannot be directly used for further processing. As the subject is exposed to emotion stimulation based on the visual inputs for a specific duration, the resulting emotional reaction would be a time-varying one. It is essential therefore to identify the duration of peak activity of the brain and extract the features only for that duration so as to enhance the classification results. To achieve this, the recording is started exactly one minute after the start of experiment, which gives enough time to simulate the emotions of the participants using the image slides corresponding to the particular emotion. Also, to avoid dealing with large data, only 15 seconds of data with 512 samples per second are considered, thereby reducing the data size to just $15 \times 512 = 7680$ samples, as illustrated in Figure 9-3. Figure 9-3 shows the signal for the entire duration of recording with the signal in the peak period of brain activity indicated in red, and Figure 9-4 shows this part separately.

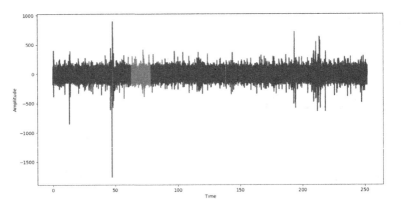

Figure 9-3. *Sample EEG signal for the entire recording duration*

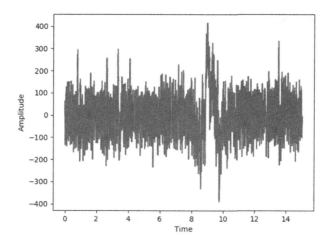

Figure 9-4. EEG signal extracted during peak activity of brain

Features Taken from the Brain Wave Signal

EEG signals are a rich source of brain function information. To get meaningful information from EEG signals, different attributes of the signals need to be extracted. A total of 9 different time domain attributes are extracted from the EEG signals, and these features are illustrated as follows.

The latency to amplitude ratio (LAR) is defined as the ratio of the maximum signal time to the maximum signal amplitude; see Equation 9-1.

$$LAR = \frac{t_{s\,max}}{S_{max}} \qquad (9\text{-}1)$$

Here, $t_{smax} = \{t \mid s(t) = s_{max}\}$ is the time where the maximum signal value occurs, and $s_{max} = \max\{s(t)\}$ is the maximum signal value.

The peak to peak signal value (PP) is defined as the difference between the maximum signal value and the minimum signal value and is shown in Equation 9-2.

$$S_{pp} = S_{max} - S_{min} \qquad (9\text{-}2)$$

177

Here, s_{max} and s_{min} are the signal maximum and minimum values, respectively.

The peak to peak time window (PPT) is defined as the difference between the maximum signal time and the minimum signal time and is shown in Equation 9-3.

$$t_{pp} = t_{s\,max} - t_{s\,min}$$ (9-3)

Here, $t_{s\,max}$ and $t_{s\,min}$ are the times at which the maximum and minimum signal values occur.

The peak to peak slope (PPS) is defined as the ratio of peak to peak signal value (PP) to the peak to peak time value (PPT) and is shown in Equation 9-4.

$$S_{pps} = \frac{S_{pp}}{t_{pp}}$$ (9-4)

Here, s_{pp} is the peak to peak signal value, and t_{pp} is the peak to peak time window.

The signal power (P) is defined as the signal that exists for infinite time for constant amplitude. The signal power is shown in Equation 9-5.

$$P = \frac{1}{T}\Sigma |s(t)|^2$$ (9-5)

The mean value of signal (μ) is defined as the average of data samples between the end points of the selected area and displays the average value. The mean value of signal is given in Equation 9-6.

$$\mu = \frac{1}{N}\sum_{i=1}^{N} s[i]$$ (9-6)

where N is total number of samples in signals.

Kurtosis (K) is the sharpness of the peak of a frequency-distribution curve and is given in Equation 9-7.

$$K = \frac{m_4}{m_2} \qquad (9\text{-}7)$$

Here, m_4 and m_2 is the fourth moment and variance of signal.

Mobility (M) is defined as the ratio of first-order variance of signal to the variance of the signal and is given in Equation 9-8.

$$M = \frac{Var\big(s(t)\big)'}{Var\big(s(t)\big)} \qquad (9\text{-}8)$$

Complexity (C) is defined as the first derivative of mobility divided by mobility and is given in Equation 9-9.

$$C_\varepsilon = \frac{M_\varepsilon'}{M_\varepsilon} \qquad (9\text{-}9)$$

The Python code for all these formulas for the nine time domain features is written as a single function that is later called in the main program. This function, which takes 15 seconds of EEG signal during the peak emotional activity of brain and the corresponding time samples, is illustrated here:

```python
def eegfeat(ynew,tnew):
    from scipy.stats import kurtosis
    # latency to amplitude ratio
    smax=max(ynew)
    locmax=np.where(ynew==smax)
```

```
tsmax=tnew[locmax]
lar1=tsmax/smax
lar=lar1[0]
# peak to peak signal value
smin=min(ynew)
locmin=np.where(ynew==smax)
tsmin=tnew[locmin]
spp=smax-smin
# peak to peak time window.
tpp1=tsmax+tsmin
tpp=tpp1[0]
# peak to peak slope
spps=spp/tpp
# mean value of signal
m=np.mean(ynew)
# kurtosis
k=kurtosis(ynew)
# mobility and complexity
n=ynew.shape[0]
dynew=np.diff(ynew)
ddynew=np.diff(dynew)
mx2=np.mean(np.power(ynew,2))
mdx2=np.mean(np.power(dynew,2))
mddx2=np.mean(np.power(ddynew,2))
mob=mdx2/mx2
complexity=np.sqrt(mddx2/(mdx2-mob))
mobility=np.sqrt(mob)
# signal power
tt=np.power(ynew,2)
s=0
```

```
for i in np.arange(0,tt.shape[0]):
s=s+tt[i]
signalpower=s/ynew.shape[0]
feat = [lar, spp, tpp, spps, m, k, complexity, mobility,
signalpower]
return feat
```

Unstructured Data to Structured Dataset

Now that we have a function to extract features from the EEG signal, the next step is to develop the code to get a structured dataset. First, the EEG signals of all 15 participants corresponding to three different emotions are loaded one by one using the pd.read_csv function inside a for loop. After an EEG signal is loaded as a dataframe, the timestamp is removed first, and then the amplitude values in the remaining column are converted to a NumPy array. The array obtained in each iteration is then stacked to a new variable thereby providing a final array consisting of 45 columns corresponding to the 45 different EEG signals. Then each column of this array is passed to the eegfeat function created earlier that provides nine features corresponding to each column (each signal) there by providing a final feature array of size 9×45. The dataset is given in Table 9-1 and saved as emotion_data1.xls in an Excel sheet. Finally, the features are scaled using the StandardScaler and fit function in the sklearns module. This scaling works by first computing the mean and standard deviation of each feature for all the 45 signals and then subtracting the mean from all the values and dividing this difference by the standard deviation. The following code illustrates the feature extraction process:

```
import pandas as pd
import numpy as np
from sklearn.preprocessing import StandardScaler
F=512
```

```
a=np.zeros([(75*F)-(60*F),1])
for i in np.arange(1,4):
    for j in np.arange(1,16):
        filename = 'G:/Anand-EEG/EEG Database/Dataset/
                    user'+str(j)+'_'+str(i)+'.csv'
        s=pd.read_csv(filename)
        s.drop('Time',inplace = True, axis=1)
        s1=s[' Value'][60*F:75*F]
        a=np.column_stack((a,s1.to_numpy()))
a=np.delete(a,0,1)
tnew=np.linspace(0,15,a.shape[0])
features=np.zeros([9,45])
for i in np.arange(0,a.shape[1]):
    parameters=eegfeat(a[:,i],tnew)
    for j in np.arange(0,features.shape[0]):
        features[j,i]=parameters[j]
scaler = StandardScaler()
features=scaler.fit(features)
```

Table 9-1. *Human Emotion Dataset Features*

LAR	PP	PPT	PPS	Power	Mean	Kurtosis	Mobility	Complexity	Label
0.016024	678	11.18505	60.61663	-0.04396	6.543546	0.864608	0.272718	3095.76805	'Happy'
0.021638	805	17.95937	44.8234	-0.13187	1.147168	0.908352	0.323672	8861.53844	'Happy'
0.013645	1156	18.50241	62.47835	-0.13599	11.54561	0.909418	0.253198	5615.14591	'Happy'
0.020861	913	20.6941	44.11885	-0.19559	4.77647	0.869794	0.274665	7488.51785	'Happy'
0.027464	1051	29.44133	35.69811	0.073972	-0.04979	0.920326	0.739543	17478.1566	'Happy'
0.003051	1056	3.215262	328.4335	0.555873	-0.70347	0.829795	0.648545	26836.2039	'Happy'
0.009142	708	5.996875	118.0615	-1.4202	1.801014	0.807949	0.203007	5224.79068	'Happy'
0.044871	577	27.64032	20.8753	0.774106	5.355427	0.872217	0.221742	3616.08585	'Happy'
0.025742	1017	25.99948	39.11617	-0.02595	15.2165	0.909882	0.275513	4281.25747	'Happy'
0.037152	595	19.31892	30.79882	0.490321	2.851322	0.908083	0.295561	3403.52707	'Happy'
0.017313	940	15.40826	61.00625	0.107773	0.582757	0.772671	0.179429	14818.1692	'Happy'
0.015074	1626	22.58107	72.00723	-2.5419	2.847854	0.813119	0.216638	25075.0479	'Happy'
0.034336	812	24.72197	32.84528	0.310597	9.089532	0.908852	0.326948	3481.33912	'Happy'
0.012292	918	12.0211	76.36575	-0.1356	12.5699	0.88202	0.218335	4644.36149	'Happy'

(continued)

Table 9-1. (*continued*)

LAR	PP	PPT	PPS	Power	Mean	Kurtosis	Mobility	Complexity	Label
0.001722	3060	4.613882	663.2159	-0.01663	34.31637	0.827843	0.097603	30433.0506	'Happy'
0.018688	402	8.89569	45.19043	0.032993	4.738717	0.882602	0.423034	1124.38087	'Fear'
0.040525	579	26.50345	21.84621	0.254913	2.882232	0.906008	0.304122	4124.12924	'Fear'
0.020358	1517	21.62	70.1665	-0.11243	40.33238	0.916268	0.270259	7677.61001	'Fear'
0.057451	383	22.63576	16.92013	0.012297	0.515585	0.915245	0.524744	1586.28054	'Fear'
0.02732	735	23.11238	31.80113	-0.4819	2.371013	0.840896	0.430931	5550.91016	'Fear'
0.010694	1567	16.40448	95.52269	0.170683	-0.28034	0.906462	0.697989	35493.9062	'Fear'
0.027347	378	10.88423	34.72915	0.02714	0.021038	0.779173	0.311332	2214.34304	'Fear'
0.038418	717	29.58198	24.23773	-0.75375	2.735193	0.886821	0.155092	7204.2341	'Fear'
0.023423	1115	25.76507	43.27564	-0.3602	2.435107	0.860817	0.38882	12420.8748	'Fear'
0.002859	4420	12.57976	351.358	4.408442	5.755933	0.6055	0.123552	296978.069	'Fear'
0.025219	971	24.71416	39.28922	-0.08303	1.857694	0.766682	0.165919	11425.814	'Fear'
0.015038	2516	21.53405	116.8382	-2.2011	30.45224	0.93143	0.384335	22246.7576	'Fear'
0.017566	833	14.40422	57.83028	-0.42794	2.695262	0.842994	0.172786	8374.92373	'Fear'
0.019647	935	20.27608	46.11346	0.316469	3.61666	0.9339	0.34069	8803.85773	'Fear'

0.006667	1404	12.45475	112.7281	0.157155	27.96396	0.854443	0.211712	6280.25928	'Fear'
0.01213	992	14.45891	68.6082	-0.29278	7.918369	0.826067	0.157843	8135.80814	'Sad'
0.016787	1187	19.33846	61.38029	0.17177	5.274371	0.862185	0.195176	16224.2062	'Sad'
0.025382	1017	24.46803	41.56444	0.228652	14.78168	0.863634	0.195593	5841.32003	'Sad'
0.012709	1524	18.68212	81.57532	-0.20364	19.9148	0.873179	0.190631	10495.4369	'Sad'
0.047707	499	24.13986	20.6712	0.102337	3.259416	0.864654	0.309553	2265.85228	'Sad'
0.006046	1933	10.67717	181.0405	0.758343	2.349937	1.003761	0.682323	24010.3048	'Sad'
0.020863	1305	24.40943	53.46295	0.003427	0.833297	0.768599	0.488095	22671.4565	'Sad'
0.020863	1305	24.40943	53.46295	0.003427	0.833297	0.768599	0.488095	22671.4565	'Sad'
0.033872	863	25.47207	33.88025	0.105906	9.95777	0.858691	0.220224	5482.11932	'Sad'
0.02912	535	15.78331	33.89658	-0.01854	0.234449	0.896769	0.619883	4619.19634	'Sad'
0.000649	5070	3.141034	1614.118	-4.11542	6.964611	0.795685	0.173283	231638.996	'Sad'
0.015449	856	14.58393	58.69474	0.157962	1.97371	0.786113	0.225146	6764.73669	'Sad'
0.005224	3800	20.26826	187.4852	0.570607	22.94134	0.791691	0.094596	63679.0805	'Sad'
0.016787	1187	19.33846	61.38029	0.17177	5.274371	0.862185	0.195176	16224.2062	'Sad'
0.008937	494	4.879542	101.239	0.109418	0.696421	0.769311	0.304871	3185.67894	'Sad'

Exploratory Data Analysis from the EEG Data

To read the emotion_data.xls file, use the following code:

```
import pandas as pd
emotion_data= pd.read_excel('\file_path\emotion_data1.xls')
To show the keys and first 5 dataset using the below code
print(emotion_data.keys())
Output:
Index(['LAR', 'PP', 'PPT', 'PPS', 'Power', 'Mean', 'Kurtosis',
'Mobility', 'Complexity', 'Label'], dtype='object')
print(emotion_data.head(5))
Output:
    LAR        PP    PPT       PPS         ...  Kurtosis  Mobility
Complexity  Label
0   0.016024  678  11.18505  60.61663  ...  0.864608  0.272718
3095.76805  'Happy'
1   0.021638  805  17.95937  44.82340  ...  0.908352  0.323672
8861.53844  'Happy'
2   0.013645  1156 18.50241  62.47835  ...  0.909418  0.253198
5615.14591  'Happy'
3   0.020861  913  20.69410  44.11885  ...  0.869794  0.274665
7488.51785  'Happy'
4   0.027464  1051 29.44133  35.69811  ...  0.920326  0.739543
17478.15660 'Happy'
```

By using the following code, the final five data points can be viewed:

```
print(emotion_data.tail(5))
        LAR      PP        PPT  ...  Mobility
   Complexity       Label
40  0.000649  5070   3.141034  ...  0.173283
   231638.99600     'Sad'
41  0.015449   856  14.583930  ...  0.225146
   6764.73669        'Sad'
42  0.005224  3800  20.268260  ...  0.094596
   63679.08050  'Sad'
43  0.016787  1187  19.338460  ...  0.195176
   16224.20620  'Sad'
44  0.008937   494   4.879542  ...  0.304871
   3185.67894       'Sad'
[5 rows x 10 columns]
```

To check the shape of the data, use the following code:

```
print(emotion_data.shape)
Output:
(45, 10)
```

By using the below code, the datatypes in the emotion data can be displayed.

```
print(emotion_data.dtypes)
Output:
LAR              float64
PP                 int64
PPT              float64
PPS              float64
Power            float64
Mean             float64
Kurtosis         float64
```

```
Mobility          float64
Complexity        float64
Emotion Label      object
dtype: object
```

The modifications in the dataset include dropping the columns and changing the data using the exploratory data analysis section in Chapter 8.

Figure 9-5 shows the visualization of a histogram of the mean data in the emotion dataset.

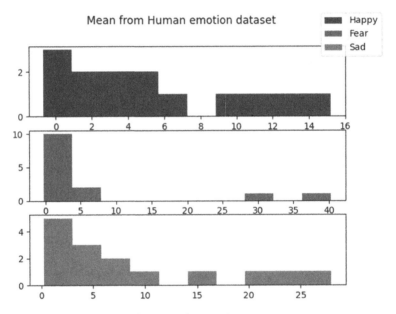

Figure 9-5. *Histogram of mean for each emotion*

Classifying the Emotion Using Learning Models

The next step after extracting the features is to apply a classification algorithm to identify the emotion corresponding to the signals. Since we are already aware of the emotions corresponding to each of the signals we have used, it is obviously better to go for a supervised learning algorithm for classification. Before that, another important task is to split our data into training and testing data. Out of the 15 signals for each emotion, let's consider the data corresponding to first 12 signals for training and the data corresponding to the remaining 3 signals for testing. Also, the labels corresponding to the training and testing data should be created. For this, we are going to label the emotion *happy* as 1, *fear* as 2, and *sad* as 3. This splitting of data as well as the labels is illustrated in the following code:

```
m1=np.ones((15,),dtype=int)
ids=np.concatenate((m1,2*m1,3*m1),axis=0)
x_train=np.concatenate((features[:,0:12],features[:,15:27],
features[:,30:42]),axis=1)
x_test=np.concatenate((features[:,12:15],features[:,27:30],
features[:,42:45]),axis=1)
y_train=np.concatenate((ids[0:12],ids[15:27],ids[30:42]))
y_test=np.concatenate((ids[12:15],ids[27:30],ids[42:45]))
```

   i.   k-NN

Let's first use the k-NN algorithm to classify the emotions based on the data. k-NN is a simple supervised machine learning algorithm that categorizes the available data and assigns new data to a particular category based on a similarity score. The k-NN algorithm works by finding the distance between the test data and the training data. After finding the distance to each training data, the training data is sorted in ascending order of the distance values. In this ordered data, the first k data is selected, and the algorithm will assign the most frequent label occurring in this to the test data. The Euclidean distance is the most commonly used distance measure for the k-NN algorithm, and the distance between two data points, x_i and y_i, is given by the following expression:

$$\text{Euclidean distance} = \sqrt{\sum_{i=1}^{k}(x_i - y_i)^2}$$

The k-NN classification is implemented using the KNeighborsClassifier package in the sklearn Python module. The emotion classification code using this package is illustrated here:

```
from sklearn.neighbors import KNeighborsClassifier
from sklearn.metrics import confusion_matrix, classification_
report
classifier = KNeighborsClassifier(n_neighbors=16)
classifier.fit(x_train.T, y_train)
y_pred = classifier.predict(x_test.T)
cm=confusion_matrix(y_test, y_pred)
print("confusion matrix\n",cm)
print("Accuracy:",(sum(np.diagonal(cm))/9)*100)
Output:
        confusion matrix
        [[1 0 2]
        [1 2 0]
         [2 0 1]]
Accuracy: 44.44444444444444
```

The parameter n_neighbors in the previous code indicates the value of k, which we have selected as 16. Therefore, 16 neighbors are considered for making the classification decision. First, the distance between the test data and all the other training data is computed. Then the training data points are sorted in ascending order of the computed distance. In the sorted data, the labels corresponding to the first 16 data are considered, and the label that occurs more out of the 16 is assigned to the test data. This is repeated for all nine test signals (three for each emotion), and the results are displayed using a confusion matrix, which could be better understood using the information in Table 9-2.

Table 9-2. *Confusion Matrix for Emotion Classification Using k-NN*

	Happy	Fear	Sad
Happy	1	0	2
Fear	1	2	0
Sad	2	0	1

In the confusion matrix, the row headers can be treated as inputs, and column headers can be treated as outputs. For instance, if we consider the first row, only one of the three EEG signals corresponding to the "happy" emotion is identified correctly, and the remaining two signals are wrongly classified as "sad" emotion. Similarly, in the second row, two signals corresponding to the "fear" emotion are classified correctly, and in the third row, one signal corresponding to the "sad" emotion is identified correctly. To understand better, the diagonal elements in the confusion matrix represent the data that is classified correctly, and the remaining elements indicate misclassification. In total, four out of the nine test signals are classified correctly. giving the system an accuracy of 44.44 percent.

Case Study 2: Data Science for Image Data

Though digital equipment available today can capture images at a higher resolution and with more details than human vision, computers can only treat those images as an array of numerical values that represents colors. *Computer vision* refers to the techniques that can enable computers to understand digital images and videos. Computer vision systems can be thought of as a replication of the human vision system, enabling computers to process images and videos in the same way humans do. Computer vision systems are used in many applications such as face recognition, autonomous vehicles, healthcare, security, augmented reality, etc.

The first step in any computer vision system is to capture the images of interest. This can be done by many means such as cameras, microscopes, X-ray machines, radar, etc., depending on the nature of application. The captured raw images, however, cannot be used directly and require further processing. The raw images may not be of the desired quality due to the noise introduced by various reasons. It is therefore essential to enhance the captured raw images before further processing. To enable the computer to learn from the images, it is sometimes essential to extract useful information from the image using analysis techniques. In this section, we will see how to capture images using a camera interfaced to a Raspberry Pi board and discuss the steps involved in preparing the raw images for further processing.

The first step is to interface a USB web camera to our Raspberry Pi board, as shown in Figure 9-6.

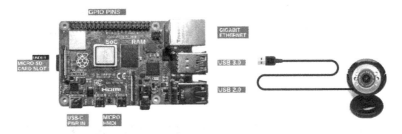

Figure 9-6. *Raspberry Pi with webcam*

To do this, we have to enable SSH and Camera in the Pi configuration settings. Secure Shell (SSH) can help to connect with the Raspberry Pi remotely over your local network, whereas enabling the Camera configuration can help to interface a webcam with the Pi board. This can be done with the following steps:

1. Type the command `sudo raspi-config` in the Terminal window of your Raspberry Pi OS. This will open the Software Configuration Tool window, as shown in Figure 9-7.

2. Go to Interfacing Options, as shown in Figure 9-8,
    and enable both SSH and Camera.

3. Reboot the Raspberry Pi device.

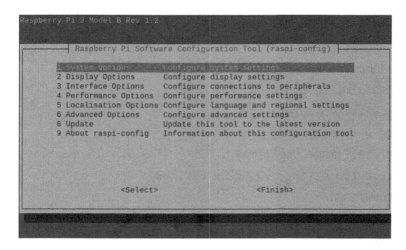

Figure 9-7. Software Configuration Tool window

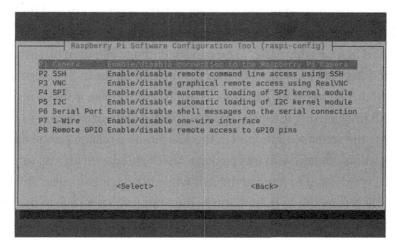

Figure 9-8. Interfacing options for enabling Camera and SSH

Once the reboot is completed, run the lsusb command in the Terminal window and check whether the connected USB webcam is listed. Then open the Python IDE and type the following code to capture and save an image using the webcam:

```
import cv2
import pandas as pd
import numpy as np
import matplotlib.pyplot as plt
camera=cv2.VideoCapture( )
ret, img = camera.read( )
cv2.imwrite('image.png',img)
img= cv2.cvtColor(img,cv2.COLOR_BGR2RGB)
plt.imshow(img)
plt.axis('off')
plt.show( )
```

As shown in the code, the OpenCV package is used to work with images in Python. To capture an image, a VideoCapture object is created first. The read( ) function is used to capture the image using the created object and then stored in a variable 'img'. The captured image can then be saved using the imwrite( ) function. OpenCV displays an image in BGR format instead of the standard RGB format. Therefore, the image is first converted to an RGB image using the cv2.color function before displaying. To display the image, the imshow( ) function in the Matplotlib package can be used. Since the plots created with this package are enabled with an axis value by default, it is essential to remove the axis while displaying images. This can be done by setting the axis function in the Matplotlib package to the off state. Figure 9-9 shows a sample image captured using the previous code.

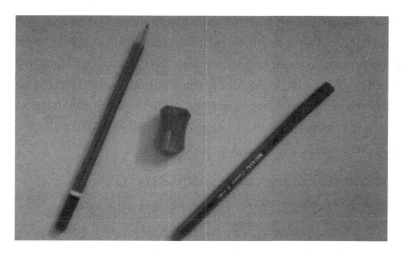

Figure 9-9. *Image captured using a webcam interfaced to the Raspberry Pi board*

Exploratory Image Data Analysis

The image shows a few stationary objects lying on white paper. To understand the acquired image data, it would be better to print the data type and size of the image, as illustrated here:

```
print(type(img))
print(img.shape)
Output:
        <class 'numpy.ndarray'>
        (719, 1206, 3)
```

The captured image is a NumPy array. The image captured using the webcam is usually in RGB form where there are three planes of pixels: Red, Blue, and Green. In other words, each pixel in the image is composed of three values that represent the proportion of red, blue, and green thereby leading to various colors in the visible spectrum. The number 3 in the shape of the image printed indicates the three planes; i.e., the image is

composed of three planes corresponding to RGB, each with a size of 719×
1206 pixels. In many applications, other details such as edges, shapes,
etc., in the image are more important than the color information. For
instance, if our objective is to identify the stationary objects in the given
image, the shape of the objects would be more important than the color. In
such cases, the three-plane RGB image can be converted to a single-plane
grayscale image using the following code:

```
gray = cv2.cvtColor(img, cv2.COLOR_BGR2GRAY)
plt.imshow(gray,cmap= 'gray')
plt.axis('off')
plt.show( )
print(gray.shape)
Output:
    (719, 1206)
```

Figure 9-10 shows a single-plane grayscale image where the colors
in the image are removed. This can be seen from the size of the image
printed in the previous code. Now the size of the grayscale image is just
719×1206 in a single plane. In some cases, the captured image may have
some missing values caused by defects in the image sensor. These values
may be reflected in the grayscale image as well, and these values can be
detected and treated by converting the image to a dataframe, as illustrated
here:

```
df=pd.DataFrame(gray)
s=df.isnull( ).sum( ).sum( )
print(s)
if s!=0:
    df=df.ffill(axis=0)
gray=df.to_numpy( )
Output:
    0
```

The isnull( ) function can be used to detect the presence of missing values along the rows and columns of the image. The sum( ) function can be used to count the number of missing values in the dataframe along rows and columns. If the result of the sum( ) function is not equal to zero, then the image consists of missing values, and they can be treated using the ffill( ) function, which replaces each missing value with the pixel above it. This method of forward filling or backward filling will not cause any visible changes in the image because pixel values are often closely placed in an image except at edges in the image. As shown from the previous code, the number of missing values is 0; i.e., there are no missing values in the image. Once the image is checked and treated for missing values, the dataframe can be converted back to a NumPy array using to_ numpy( ) in Pandas. Since the pixel values are closely placed, there may be repetition of same pixel values at many regions in the image. Because of this property, identification of duplicate values is irrelevant in the case of the image data.

Figure 9-10. Image converted to grayscale

Using a USB webcam or the Pi camera in natural lighting may often result in poor-quality images. So, the next step after treating missing values is to plot the histogram of the image. The histogram plot will give an idea about the contrast of the image, as shown in Figure 9-11. This is illustrated in the following code:

```
plt.hist(gray.ravel( ),bins=256)
plt.xlabel('bins')
plt.ylabel('No of pixels')
plt.show( )
```

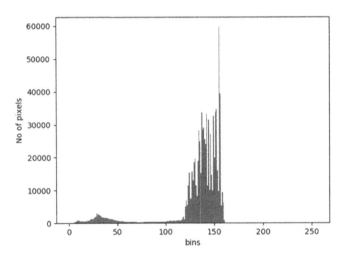

Figure 9-11. *Histogram of the grayscale image*

The pixel values in a grayscale image range from 0 (representing black) to 255 (representing white). The hist( ) function in the previous code plots a bar chart of the count of each pixel value in this range. This plot gives insight about the contrast of the image that we are dealing with. Figure 9-7 shows the histogram of our grayscale image. It can be seen that the majority of the pixels are in the range (120,160). If the spread of pixels is concentrated in the lower bins, then we have a low-contrast image, and vice versa. So, depending on this plot, a decision can be made as to whether the image needs contrast adjustment.

The other cause for the poor quality of images may be the presence of noise induced by various factors. These noises can be visually perceived, while observing the captured images, in the form of grains. In such cases, these noises have to be removed before going for further processing. There are many different kinds of noises such as Gaussian noise, salt and pepper noise, etc., and there are many different types of filters that can be used to remove those noises that are beyond the scope of this book. Let's just look at one particular filter used often in image processing called the *averaging filter*. It is a low-pass filter that can be used to remove high-frequency content from a digital image. This filtering works by passing a kernel of particular size, say 3×3, across the dimensions of the image, taking the average of all the pixels under the kernel area and replacing the central element with this average. The overall effect is to create a blurring effect. The following code illustrates the implementation of averaging filter to our image. Figure 9-12 shows the image obtained after filtering.

```
blur=cv2.blur(gray,(3,3))
plt.imshow(blur)
plt.axis('off')
plt.show( )
```

Figure 9-12. *Image obtained by average filtering*

Preparing the Image Data for Model

Once the preprocessing steps are completed, the next step is to analyze or prepare the image for a learning model. This can be done in two ways. The first way is to extract features that represent useful information and use them for modeling. The features extracted may be another transformed image, or they may be attributes extracted from the original image. There are numerous features that can be extracted from an image, and the selection of a particular feature depends on the nature of our application. A discussion of these numerous features is beyond the scope of this book. Instead, we will discuss one particular feature: edge detection.

Edges represent the high-frequency content in an image. Canny edge detection is an algorithm that uses a multistage approach to detect a wide range of edges in images. It can be implemented in Python by using the Canny( ) function in OpenCV, as illustrated in the following code. Figure 9-13 shows the image after the edge detection process.

```
edge_img=cv2.Canny(gray,100,200)
plt.imshow(edge_img,cmap='gray')
plt.axis('off')
plt.show( )
```

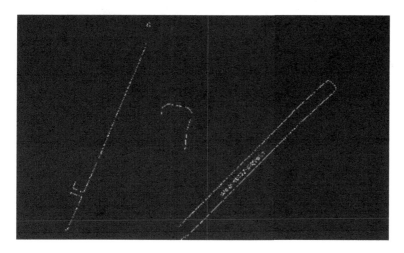

Figure 9-13. *Image after edge detection*

The second way is to directly feed the image to a deep learning model. Deep learning is a popular machine learning approach that is being increasingly used for analyzing and learning from images. This approach can directly learn the useful information from the image and does not require any feature extraction. The image may be resized to a different shape and then fed to the learning model, or the image array may be converted to a one-dimensional vector and then fed to the model.

Object Detection Using a Deep Neural Network

Object detection is a technique for identifying the objects in the real world like a chair, book, car, TV, flowers, animals, humans, etc., from an image or video. This technique detects, identifies, and recognizes multiple objects in an image for better understanding or for extracting the information from a real-world environment. Object detection plays a major role in computer vision applications like autonomous vehicles, surveillance, automation in industries, and assistive devices for visually impaired people. Many modules are available in the Python environment for object detection, and they are as follows:

> Feature-based object detection
>
> Viola Jones object detection
>
> SVM classification with HOG features
>
> Deep learning object detection
>
> Single-shot multibox detector (SSD) object detection
>
> You Only Look Once (YOLO) model object detection
>
> Region-based convolutional neural network (R-CNN)
>
> Faster R-CNN

Here, we have used a single-shot multibox detector to identify the multiple objects in an image or video. Single-shot multibox detectors were proposed by C. Szegedy et al. in November 2016. SSD can be explained as follows:

> *Single shot*: In this stage, localization and classification of the image are done with the help of a single forward-pass network.
>
> *Multibox*: This represents drawing the bounding boxes for multiple objects in an image.
>
> *Detector*: This is an object detector that classifies the objects in an image or video.

Figure 9-14 shows the architecture of a single-shot multibox detector.

In the architecture, the dimension of the input image is considered as 300×300×3. The VGG-16 architecture is used as a base network, and the fully connected networks are discarded. The VGG-16 architecture is popular and has a strong classification ability with the transfer learning technique. Here, a part of the convolutional layers of the VGG-16 architecture is used in the earlier stages. A detailed explanation of SSD is available at https://towardsdatascience.com/understanding-ssd-multibox-real-time-object-detection-in-deep-learning-495ef744fab.

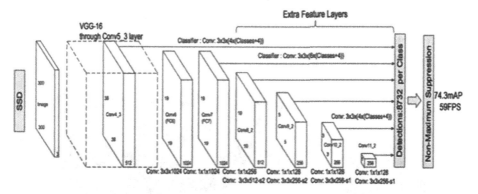

Figure 9-14. *Architecture of single-shot multibox detector (https:// towardsdatascience.com/understanding-ssd-multibox-real-time-object-detection-in-deep-learning-495ef744fab)*

The multibox architecture is a technique for identifying the bounding box coordinates and is based on two loss functions such as confidence loss and location loss. Confidence loss uses a categorical entropy for measuring the confidence level of identifying the objects for the bounding box. Location loss measures the distance of the bounding box, which is away from the object in the image. For measuring the distance, the L2 norm is used. The multibox loss can be measured with the help of the following equation:

$$\text{Multi-box loss} = \text{confidence Loss} + \alpha * \text{Location Loss}$$

This gives information about how far the bounding box landed from the predicted objects. The following code implements the SSD configure file with the DNN weights for detecting the objects in COCO names. The SSD configure file (i.e., `ssd_mobilenet_v3_large_coco_2020_01_14.pbtxt`) with the DNN weights (i.e., `frozen_inference_graph.pb`) for detecting the objects in COCO names can be downloaded from `https://github.com/AlekhyaBhupati/Object_Detection_Using_openCV`.

COCO names are called common objects in this context, and the dataset for the COCO names is available at the official website: `https://cocodataset.org/#home`. COCO has segmented common objects such as chair, car, animals, humans, etc., and these segmented images can be used to train the deep neural network. See Figure 9-15 and Figure 9-16.

***Figure 9-15.** Input image for object identification*

Here's the code:

```
import cv2
thres = 0.5# Threshold to detect object
cap = cv2.VideoCapture(0)
cap.set(3,1280)
cap.set(4,720)
cap.set(10,70)
classNames= []
classFile = 'coco.names'
with open(classFile,'rt') as f:
    classNames = f.read().rstrip('\n').split('\n')

configPath = 'ssd_mobilenet_v3_large_coco_2020_01_14.pbtxt'
weightsPath = 'frozen_inference_graph.pb'

net = cv2.dnn_DetectionModel(weightsPath,configPath)
net.setInputSize(320,320)
net.setInputScale(1.0/ 127.5)
net.setInputMean((127.5, 127.5, 127.5))
net.setInputSwapRB(True)
print('1st done')
while True:
    success, img = cap.read()
    classIds, confs, bbox = net.detect(img, confThreshold=thres)
    print(classIds, bbox)
     if len(classIds) != 0:
        for classId, confidence,box in zip(classIds.
        flatten(),confs.flatten(),bbox):
            cv2.rectangle(img,box,color=(0,255,0),thickness=2)
            cv2.putText(img,classNames[classId-1].upper(),
            (box[0]+10,box[1]+30),
                        cv2.FONT_HERSHEY_COMPLEX,1,(0,255,0),2)
```

```
        cv2.putText(img,str(round(confidence*100,2)),(box[0
        ]+200,box[1]+30),
                        cv2.FONT_HERSHEY_COMPLEX,1,
                        (0,255,0),2)
cv2.imshow("Output",img)
# Hit 'q' on the keyboard to quit!
```

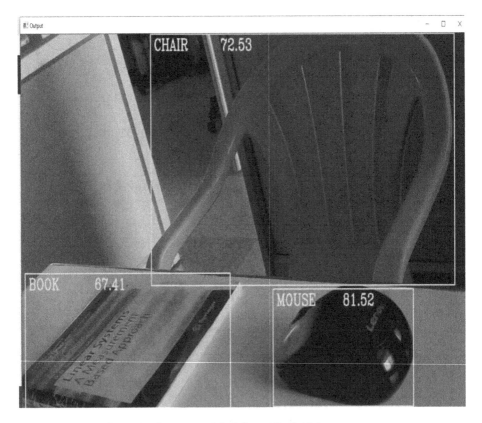

Figure 9-16. *Output image with identified objects*

When the code is executed, the frames in the video from the webcam are captured using the OpenCV capture functions. Then, each and every frame is inserted into the already trained SSD-DNN model for identifying the objects. The SSD-DNN model classifies the objects based on the COCO names and creates a bounding box on the detected images with a COCO name label and accuracy. The video file of Figure 9-15 was fed as the input to the previous program. The figure has the objects such as a chair, a book, and a mouse. From Figure 9-16, it can clearly be concluded that the SSD-based DNN model identifies the three objects with an accuracy of 72.53 percent for the chair, 67.41 percent for the book, and 81.52 percent for the mouse.

Case Study 3: Industry 4.0

Industry 4.0 represents the fourth revolution in the manufacturing industry. The first revolution in industry (i.e., Industry 1.0) was the creation of mechanical energy with the help of steam power to increase the productivity in assembly lines. The second revolution (i.e., Industry 2.0) incorporated electricity into the assembly line to improve productivity. The third revolution (i.e., Industry 3.0) incorporated computers for automating the industrial process. Currently, Industry 4.0 is adopting computers, data analysis, and machine learning tools for making intelligent decisions or monitoring the process with the help of data that is acquired with sensors. The Internet of Things (IoT) has recently played a major role in acquiring data and transmitting it for remote access.

Figure 9-17 describes the basic process flow in Industry 4.0. Initially, the physical system's data is collected with the help of sensors and made into a digital record. Then the digital record of the physical systems is sent to a server system for real-time data processing and analysis. The data science techniques are applied in this stage for preprocessing and preparing the data. Then modern learning algorithms can be used for intelligent decision-making by predicting the output with the learned model. Moreover, visualization techniques are used to monitor the real-time data of the physical systems. Here, the Raspberry Pi can be used as a server or a localized cloud for real-time data processing.

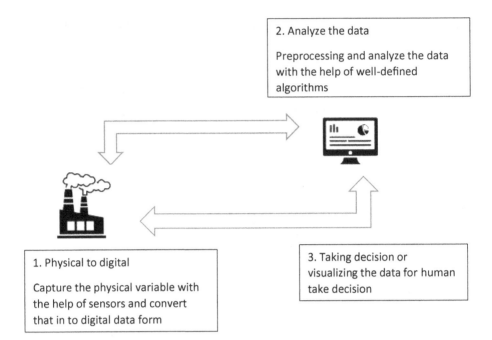

Figure 9-17. *Industry 4.0 block diagram*

Raspberry Pi as a Localized Cloud for Industry 4.0

To implement Industry 4.0, a sophisticated computer is required to connect the devices, collect the data, and process the data. The collected data can be stored in a cloud service for further processing. However, these days, subscriptions of cloud services are costlier and suitable for highly profitable companies. Small-scale companies will want to implement a localized cloud for real-time processing. Further, a localized cloud approach can provide data security because it's on-site and attackers are not able to invade via remote access.

As discussed in Chapter 3, the Raspberry Pi can act as a localized cloud that can connect sensors, IoT devices, other nearby computers, and mobile phones, as shown in Figure 9-18. Sophisticated computers also can act as a localized cloud, but they occupy a large space. Also, it is difficult to implement the computers in remote areas. The Raspberry Pi has the advantage of occupying less space and can be implemented in remote areas. Based on this, the Raspberry Pi is used as a localized cloud for the Industry 4.0 framework, as shown in Figure 9-19.

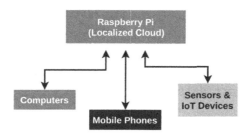

Figure 9-18. *The Raspberry Pi as a localized cloud*

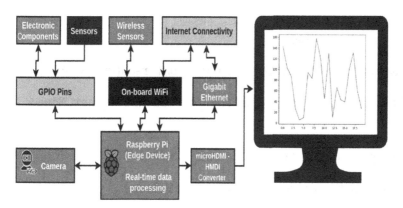

Figure 9-19. *Industry 4.0 framework with the Raspberry Pi*

There are three modules available in the Industry 4.0 framework with the Raspberry Pi. The modules are collecting the data from the sensors, collecting the information using cameras, and connecting the Raspberry Pi with other computers.

Collecting Data from Sensors

We will use the temperature and humidity sensor to measure the temperature and humidity. Connect the DHT 11/22 sensor module to the Raspberry Pi, as shown in Chapter 3. The following code collects the temperature and humidity percentage for 100 seconds and stores the collected data as a CSV file.

```python
import Adafruit_DHT
import time
from datetime import datetime

DHT_SENSOR = Adafruit_DHT.DHT11
DHT_PIN = 17

data = []

while _ in range(100):

    humidity, temperature = Adafruit_DHT.read(DHT_SENSOR, DHT_PIN)

    if humidity is not None and temperature is not None:

now = datetime.now()
dt_string = now.strftime("%d/%m/%Y %H:%M:%S")

data.append(dt_string,humidity,temperature)

    time.sleep(60*5)

df = pd.DataFrame(data)
df.to_csv('data.csv',index=None,header=None)
```

The CSV file would look like Table 9-3.

Table 9-3. *Timestamped Data from the Humidity and Temperature Sensors*

17/05/2020 01:05:14	26.24	69.91
17/05/2020 01:10:14	26.24	70.65
17/05/2020 01:15:14	26.22	68.87
17/05/2020 01:20:14	26.15	70.11
17/05/2020 01:25:14	26.11	69.02

Preparing the Industry Data in the Raspberry Pi

We will use a dataset consisting of two columns of data recorded from the temperature and humidity sensor connected to a Raspberry Pi board; the data was recorded every 5 minutes over a duration of 28 hours. So, the dataset is essentially time-series data in .csv format. It is always better to get an understanding of the dataset before doing preprocessing. Therefore, the first step will be to read the file and print the contents, as illustrated here:

```
import pandas as pd
import matplotlib.pyplot as plt
import numpy as np
dataset=pd.read_csv('datasets_384649_744229_log_temp.csv')
print(dataset.head())
Output
        Date      Time   Temperature      Humidity
0   3/14/19  19:33:07         T=22.0        H=20.0
1   3/14/19  19:38:10         T=22.0        H=20.0
2   3/14/19  19:43:11         T=22.0        H=26.0
3   3/14/19  19:48:14         T=22.0        H=26.0
4   3/14/19  19:53:15         T=22.0        H=20.0
```

From the first five entries of the dataset printed, it is clear that the data needs to be cleaned before we start analyzing it. The first two columns consisting of the date and time of the entry are not needed for the analysis, and hence those columns can be dropped. The third and fourth columns consisting of the actual data are a mix of string and numbers. We have to filter out these inappropriate values and convert the dataset from string to float. These two operations can be performed as illustrated here:

```
# drop the date and time column
drop=['Date','Time']
dataset.drop(drop,inplace=True,axis=1)
# remove the 'T=' and 'H=' string
dataset['Temperature']=dataset['Temperature'].str.
replace('T=','')
dataset['Humidity']=dataset['Humidity'].str.replace('H=','')
dataset=dataset.astype(float)
print(dataset.head())
Output:
     Temperature      Humidity
0          22.0          20.0
1          22.0          20.0
2          22.0          26.0
3          22.0          26.0
4          22.0          20.0
```

The next step is to check for missing data in both columns. As discussed earlier, the missing data is normally in the form of NaN, and the function isna() from the Pandas package can be used to detect the presence of such data. The function where() from the NumPy data can be used along with the function isna() to get the location of the missing values in the respective columns, as illustrated here:

```
print(np.where(dataset['Temperature'].isna()))
print(np.where(dataset['Humidity'].isna()))
Outpu:
(array([206, 207, 214, 215, 216, 217, 218, 219, 220, 221, 222,
223, 224, 225, 226, 227], dtype=int64),)
(array([206, 207, 214, 215, 216, 217, 218, 219, 220, 221, 222,
223, 224, 225, 226, 227], dtype=int64),)
```

As we can see from the previous result, there is missing data in both the temperature column and the humidity column, and the location of the missing data is the same in both columns. The next step will be to treat the missing values. The method of treating the missing values can vary depending on the nature of data. In our dataset, since we are have temperature and humidity values measured every five minutes, it is safe to assume that there will not be much variation over the range of the missing values. Therefore, the missing values can be filled using the ffill method, which stands for "forward fill" where the missing values are replaced by the values in the previous row. This can be implemented using the fillna() function in the Pandas package. After the implementation of this filling process, this can be verified by using the isna().any() function, which will return false if there are no missing values in any of the columns, as illustrated here:

```
dataset['Temperature']=dataset['Temperature'].
fillna(axis=0,method='ffill')
dataset['Humidity']=dataset['Humidity'].
fillna(axis=0,method='ffill')
print(dataset.isna().any())
Output:
    Temperature    False
    Humidity       False
    dtype: bool
```

Now that the missing values are treated, the next step is to look for outliers in the data. For this, let's use the Z-score we discussed earlier. Before computing the Z-score, the entries in the dataset should be converted to integers. The following code illustrates the detection and removal of outliers using the Z-score:

```
from scipy import stats
z=np.abs(stats.zscore(dataset))
df1=dataset[z>3]
print(df1)
dataset=dataset[(z<3).all(axis=1)]
Output:
        Temperature   Humidity
47              9.0      140.0
157            37.0       12.0
```

It can be seen from the previous illustration that there are two outliers corresponding to the row indices of 47 and 57. Rather than removing the outliers that correspond to the data points with a Z-score greater than 3, we retain all the data points with a Z-score less than 3.

Exploratory Data Analysis for the Real-Time Sensor Data

We discussed some of the fundamental plots used frequently by data scientists and demonstrated each plot with some readily available datasets. In this section, we are going to demonstrate some plots using real-time sensor data. Let's take the same temperature and humidity sensor data that we used in Chapter 5 to discuss the concepts of preparing the data. As we already went through all the data cleaning steps in that chapter, the same code is provided here for preparing the data before going for plots:

```python
import pandas as pd
import matplotlib.pyplot as plt
import numpy as np
from scipy import stats
dataset=pd.read_csv('datasets_384649_744229_log_temp.csv')
# drop the date and time column
drop=['Date','Time']
dataset.drop(drop,inplace=True,axis=1)
# remove the string  header'T=' and 'H='
dataset['Temperature']=dataset['Temperature'].str.
replace('T=','')
dataset['Humidity']=dataset['Humidity'].str.replace('H=','')
dataset=dataset.astype(float)
print('After removing inappropriate data\n',dataset.head())
# detect the location of missing data, if any
print('Missing values in temperature\n',np.
where(dataset['Temperature'].isna()))
print('Missing values in humidity\n',np.
where(dataset['Humidity'].isna()))
# filling the missing values using forward fill
dataset['Temperature']=dataset['Temperature'].
fillna(axis=0,method='ffill')
dataset['Humidity']=dataset['Humidity'].
fillna(axis=0,method='ffill')
# detect and remove outliers using z-score
z=np.abs(stats.zscore(dataset))
df1=dataset[z>3]
dataset=dataset[(z<3).all(axis=1)]
print(dataset.head())
```

Output:

After removing inappropriate data

	Temperature	Humidity
0	22.0	20.0
1	22.0	20.0
2	22.0	26.0
3	22.0	26.0
4	22.0	20.0

Missing values in temperature
(array([206, 207, 214, 215, 216, 217, 218, 219, 220, 221,
222, 223, 224, 225, 226, 227], dtype=int64),)
Missing values in humidity
(array([206, 207, 214, 215, 216, 217, 218, 219, 220, 221,
222, 223, 224, 225, 226, 227], dtype=int64),)

	Temperature	Humidity
0	22.0	20.0
1	22.0	20.0
2	22.0	26.0
3	22.0	26.0
4	22.0	20.0

Visualizing the Real-Time Sensor Data

Now that the data cleaning process is complete, the next step is to plot
the data. The type of plot to be used depends on the nature of data as well
as the requirements of the analysis procedure. Since we have taken the
measurements of temperature and humidity over a duration of 28 hours, it is
ideal to plot them with respect to time. But, to get a better understanding of
the variation of these two parameters, the average value is taken every four
hours, and these averages are plotted using a bar plot. If we want to visualize

the distribution of temperature and humidity over the entire duration rather than their variation, then the range of temperature and humidity can be divided into bins, and a count of the values in each bin can be used to make a pie chart. These three types of plots are illustrated as follows:

```python
# Taking average over every 4 hours
a=dataset.shape[0]
b=[]
c=[]
for i in np.arange(0,a-(a%12),48):
    b.append(np.mean(dataset.Temperature[i:i+47]))
    c.append(np.mean(dataset.Humidity[i:i+47]))
# Temperature vs Time over 28 hours
plt.subplot(221)
plt.plot(np.linspace(0,28,a),dataset.Temperature)
plt.title('Temperature vs Time')
# Humidity vs Time over 28 hours
plt.subplot(222)
plt.plot(np.linspace(0,28,a),dataset.Humidity)
plt.title('Humidity vs Time')
#Bar plot of average temperature over every 4 hours during the
28 hours
plt.subplot(223)
x=['1','2','3','4','5','6','7']
plt.bar(x,b)
plt.title('Average temperature over every 4 hours')
#Bar plot of average humidity over every 4 hours during the 28
hours
plt.subplot(224)
plt.bar(x,c)
plt.title('Average humidity over every 4 hours')
#Pie chart for temperature distribution
```

```
d=pd.DataFrame(dataset.Temperature.value_counts(bins=4))
plt.subplot(235)
plt.pie(d.Temperature,labels=d.index)
plt.title('Temperature distribution')
#Pie chart for humidity distribution
e=pd.DataFrame(dataset.Humidity.value_counts(bins=4))
plt.subplot(236)
plt.pie(e.Humidity,labels=e.index)
plt.title('Humidity distribution')
plt.show()
```

In Figure 9-20, the first two plots show the distribution of temperature and humidity where every sample of the data is plotted along the time axis, which is indicated in hours. We can see that the temperature and humidity are inversely proportional as expected. But the distribution over time is better expressed by taking the average of the samples every four hours and plotting the data in a bar chart, as shown in the third and fourth figures. The fifth and sixth figures show pie charts that focus on the distribution of temperature and humidity rather than their variation over time. Since the sensor data is recorded for only 28 hours, there will not be large variations in the data, and hence only four bins are used to plot the distribution. From these two figures, we can see that the temperature is mostly in the range of 15 to 20 during those 28 hours, and the humidity is mostly in the range of 19 to 25, respectively.

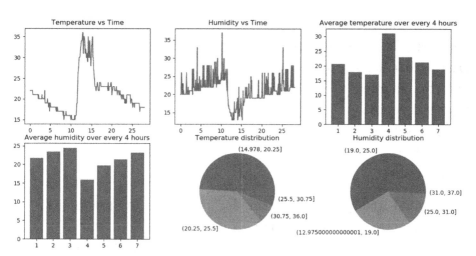

Figure 9-20. *Variation and distribution of temperature and humidity*

Report Generation by Reading Bar Codes Using Vision Cameras

Today many industries have documented their products with the help of barcodes and QR codes. Information about the product can be printed on the product for easy identification and documentation. Dedicative bar/QR code scanners are available on the market, but it requires human effort to scan the bar/QR code on the products. This may decrease productivity on the assembly line. Nowadays, vision systems are employed to automatically scan the bar/QR code on the products. This will improve productivity by eliminating the human effort and by reducing the time on the assembly line. Hence, a camera can be interfaced with the Raspberry Pi to scan the bar/QR code of the products on the assembly line.

We already discussed how to enable cameras on the Raspberry Pi in case study 2 of this chapter (refer to case study 2 for the steps to interface a webcam with the Raspberry Pi). The following code [30] continuously collects the images of the product on the assembly line, identifies the bar/QR code in the image, decodes the information in the bar/QR code, and displays the decoded information on the image screen.

```
# import the required packages
from imutils.video import VideoStream
from pyzbar import pyzbar
import argparse
import datetime
import imutils
import time
import cv2

# construct the argument parser and parse the arguments
ap = argparse.ArgumentParser()
ap.add_argument("-o", "--output", type=str, default="barcodes.csv",
    help="path to output CSV file containing barcodes")
args = vars(ap.parse_args())

# initialize the video stream and allow the camera sensor to
warm up
print("[INFO] starting video stream...")
vs = VideoStream(src=0).start()
#vs = VideoStream(usePiCamera=True).start()
time.sleep(2.0)

# open the output CSV file for writing and initialize the set of
# barcodes found thus far
csv = open(args["output"], "w")
found = set()

# loop over the frames from the video stream
while True:
    # grab the frame from the threaded video stream and resize
    it to
    # have a maximum width of 400 pixels
    frame = vs.read()
    frame = imutils.resize(frame, width=400)
```

```
# find the barcodes in the frame and decode each of the
barcodes
barcodes = pyzbar.decode(frame)
# loop over the detected barcodes
for barcode in barcodes:
    # extract the bounding box location of the barcode
    and draw
    # the bounding box surrounding the barcode on the image
    (x, y, w, h) = barcode.rect
    cv2.rectangle(frame, (x, y), (x + w, y + h), (0, 0,
    255), 2)

    # the barcode data is a bytes object so if we want to
    draw it
    # on our output image we need to convert it to a
    string first
    barcodeData = barcode.data.decode("utf-8")
    barcodeType = barcode.type

    # draw the barcode data and barcode type on the image
    text = "{} ({})".format(barcodeData, barcodeType)
    cv2.putText(frame, text, (x, y - 10),
        cv2.FONT_HERSHEY_SIMPLEX, 0.5, (0, 0, 255), 2)

    # if the barcode text is currently not in our CSV
    file, write
    # the timestamp + barcode to disk and update the set
    if barcodeData not in found:
        csv.write("{},{}\n".format(datetime.datetime.now(),
            barcodeData))
        csv.flush()
        found.add(barcodeData)
```

```
                    # show the output frame
cv2.imshow("Barcode Scanner", frame)
key = cv2.waitKey(1) & 0xFF

# if the `q` key was pressed, break from the loop
if key == ord("q"):
    break

# close the output CSV file do a bit of cleanup
print("[INFO] cleaning up...")
csv.close()
cv2.destroyAllWindows()
vs.stop()
```

The previous code acquires an image using a webcam and captures each and every frame using a while loop. Further, the frames are displayed continuously with the help of an infinite while loop. The 'q' key is used to break the infinite while loop. Then, the image acquisition can be released with the help of cap.release. In the program, each acquired frame is fed to the pyzbar module to identify the bar/QR code in the image and also to decode the data in the bar/QR code [30]. The decoded information is displayed in the corresponding frame. Figure 9-21 shows the output of the program.

Figure 9-21. *Output of barcode and QR code scanner*

Transmitting Files or Data from the Raspberry Pi to the Computer

In some scenarios, the data in the Raspberry Pi needs to be shared with nearby computers. Also, if the Raspberry Pi is somewhere else, it needs to be accessed via remote access. Many ways are available to transfer the data from the Raspberry Pi to other computers. One of the easiest and more efficient ways is to use the VNC viewer for sharing data and for remote access. VNC is the graphical desktop sharing application that allows you to control one system (i.e., the Raspberry Pi) from another system via remote access. This section discusses the installation procedure and usage of the VNC viewer for sharing files and controlling the Raspberry Pi from a remote desktop computer using VNC.

To install the VNC in Pi, the following code is used in the command window in the Raspberry Pi, as shown in Figure 9-22:

```
sudo apt update
sudo apt install realvnc-vnc-server realvnc-vnc-viewer
```

Figure 9-22. *Installation of the VNC viewer in the Raspberry Pi*

Meanwhile, VNC viewers need to be installed on a remote desktop computer. If the remote desktop computer has a different operating system (OS), VNC is compatible with all the OSs. After installing the VNC on the Pi, we have to enable the VNC server in the Raspberry Pi. The VNC server can be enabled graphically in the Raspberry Pi by following these steps:

1. Go to the Raspberry Pi graphical desktop, and select Menu ➤ Preferences ➤ Raspberry Pi Configuration. The Raspberry Pi Configuration window will open, as shown in Figure 9-23.

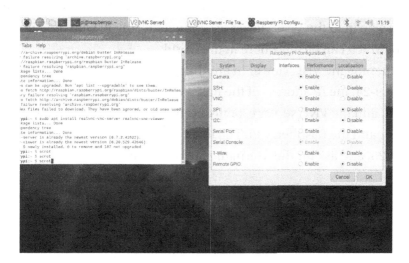

Figure 9-23. *Graphically enabling the VNC server on the Pi*

2. In the Raspberry Pi Configuration window, choose the Interfaces option and ensure that VNC is enabled. If VNC is not enabled, choose the Enable button in the window.

3. After, enabling the VNC server, click the VNC logo ◼ in the upper-right corner of the Raspberry Pi graphical desktop. The VNC viewer app window will open. In it, the IP address of the Raspberry Pi is displayed, as shown in Figure 9-8. The IP address should appear only if the Raspberry Pi is connected to a network. Here, the Raspberry Pi is connected via a WiFi network using a WiFi dongle/mobile phone hotspot.

225

These procedures are for creating a private connection between a remote desktop with the Raspberry Pi. To create a private connection, both the remote desktop and the Raspberry Pi are connected in the same network. This will create a connection only within the campus of the company. If the user wants to upload the data to the cloud, then the user needs to sign in to the VNC viewer for connecting the Pi with the remote desktop, which can be anywhere in the world.

By opening the VNC viewer in another remote desktop, as shown in Figure 9-24, the IP address of the Raspberry Pi is entered at the space provided, and the VNC server establishes the connection between the computer and the Raspberry Pi. The login window will open, as shown in Figure 9-25, and ask for the username and password.

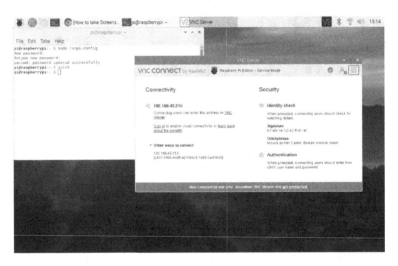

Figure 9-24. *VNC viewer in Raspberry Pi*

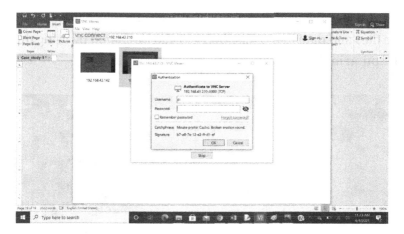

Figure 9-25. *Establishing a connection from a desktop to the Pi using the VNC viewer*

Typically, the username and password for the Raspberry Pi is *pi*. Enter **pi** for the username and password, and the Raspberry Pi desktop will appear on the remote desktop computer, as shown in Figure 9-26.

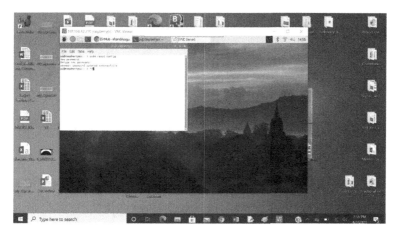

Figure 9-26. *Raspberry Pi graphical desktop on the remote computer*

227

Now, the Raspberry Pi desktop can access other computers remotely. Also, the files and data in the Raspberry Pi can be shared by using the file sharing option in the VNC viewer, as shown in Figure 9-27.

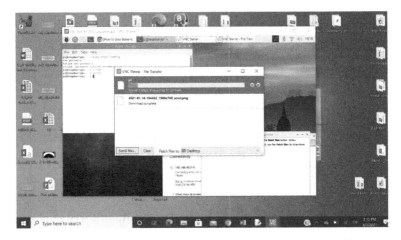

Figure 9-27. *File transfer from Raspberry Pi on remote desktop*

References

[1]   Dr. Ossama Embarak, *Data Analysis and Visualization using Python*, Apress, 2018

[2]   Peters Morgan, *Data Analysis from Scratch with Python*, AI Sciences, 2016

[3]   Dimitry Zinoviev, *Data Science Essentials in Python*, The Pragmatic Programmers, 2016

[4]   Davy Cielen, Arno D. B Meysman, Mohamed Ali, *Introducing Data Science*, Manning Publications, 2016

[5]   Laura Igual, Santi Segui, *Introduction to Data Science: A Python Approach to Concepts, Techniques and Applications*, Springer, 2017

[6]   Femi Anthony, *Mastering Pandas*, Packt Publishing, 2015

[7]   Fabio Nelli, *Python Data Analytics*, Apress, 2015

[8]   Jake VanderPlas, *Python Data Science Handbook*, O'Reilly, 2016

[9]   Wes McKinney, *Python for Data Analysis: Data Wrangling with Pandas, NumPy, and IPython*, O'Reilly, 2017

[10] John Paul Mueller, Luca Massaron, *Python for Data Science for Dummies*, John Wiley & Sons, 2015

© K. Mohaideen Abdul Kadhar and G. Anand 2021
K. M. Abdul Kadhar and G. Anand, *Data Science with Raspberry Pi*,
https://doi.org/10.1007/978-1-4842-6825-4

[11]   Dipanjan Sarkar, *Text Analytics with Python,*
       Apress, 2016

[12]   Michael Heydt, *Mastering Python Data Analysis,*
       Packt Publishing, 2016

[13]   Phuong Vo.T.H, Martin Czygan, *Getting started with*
       Python Data Analysis, Packt Publishing, 2015

[14]   Danish Haroon, *Python Machine Learning Case*
       Studies: Five Case Studies for the Data Scientist,
       Apress, 2017

[15]   Simon Monk, *Programming the Raspberry Pi:*
       Getting Started with Python, Second Edition,
       McGraw Hill Education, 2016

[16]   Richard Blum, Christine Bresnahan, *Python*
       Programming for Raspberry Pi, SAMS, 2014

[17]   "Aims and scope," IEEE Transactions on Signal
       Processing, IEEE, archived from the original on April
       17, 2012

[18]   Wes McKinney, *Python for Data Analysis: Data*
       Wrangling with Pandas, NumPy, and IPython,
       Second Edition, O'Reilly, October 2017

[19]   Chris Albon, *Machine Learning with Python*
       Cookbook: Practical Solutions from Pre-processing to
       Deep Learning, O'Reilly, March 2018

[20]   `https://towardsdatascience.com/`
       `understanding-ssd-multibox-real-time-object-`
       `detection-in-deep-learning-495ef744fab`

[21]   Joel Grus. *Data Science from Scratch: First Principles*
       with Python. O'Reilly, 2015

[22] Wes McKinney. *Python for Data Analysis*. O'Reilly, 2012

[23] Jake VanderPlas, *Python Data Science Handbook Essential Tools for Working with Data*, O'Reilly, 2017

[24] https://machinelearningmastery.com/time-series-data-visualization-with-python/

[25] https://scikit-learn.org/stable/datasets/toy_dataset.html

[26] https://www.kaggle.com/vik2012kvs/comcast-telecom-consumer-complaints

[27] John Paul Mueller, Luca Massaron, *Python for Data Science for Dummies*, John Wiley & Sons, 2015

[28] https://www.kaggle.com/yakinrubaiat/canadian-immigration-from-1980-to-2013

[29] https://towardsdatascience.com/exploratory-data-analysis-in-python-c9a77dfa39ce

[30] QR code detector, https://www.pyimagesearch.com/2018/05/21/an-opencv-barcode-and-qr-code-scanner-with-zbar/

[31] Daniel Y. Chen, *Pandas for Everyone: Python Data Analysis*, Rough Cuts, 2019

[32] Jesús Rogel-Salazar, *Data Mining and Knowledge Discovery Series*, CRC Press, 2017

[33] D. McCandless, *Information is Beautiful*. Collins, 2009

[34] H. Langtangen. *A Primer on Scientific Programming with Python: Texts in Computational Science and Engineering*, Springer, 2014

Index

A
Analog/digital signals, 80

B
Binomial distribution, 145–147
Boston housing price dataset
    corr function, 152
    features, 150
    histogram plots, 151–152
    RM/LSTAT *vs.* MEDV, 152–154
    scatter plot, 153–154

C
Camera serial interface (CSI), 74, 88
Clustering, *see* K-Means Clustering
Continuous time signal/
    continuous signal, 80

D
Data acquisition systems
    analog signal, 83
    components, 82
    digital signals, 84–85
    sensors, 82

Data analysis, 44–47
Data science
    acquisition, 5
    artificial intelligence
        techniques, 10
    automation, 10
    categorization, 1
    cloud computing, 11
    concepts, 171
    data types, 3
    edge devices, 11
    natural language processing, 11
    preparation
        analysis techniques, 9
        cleaning, 6
        duplicates, 6
        human/machines errors, 7
        missing values, 7
        modeling/algorithms, 9
        outlier data, 7–8
        processing, 6
        stage, 5
        transformation, 8
        visualization tools, 8
    processes, 4
    quantitative data, 1
    Raspberry Pi, 12

Printed in the United States
by Baker & Taylor Publisher Services